DOING RUDE THINGS
The History of the British Sex Film, 1957-1981

David McGillivray

sun tavern fields
1992

Cover design by Danusia Schejbal
Front: *Adventures of a Plumber's Mate*
Back: *The Window Dresser*

All rights reserved. No part of this publication may be reproduced, stored in a retrieval system, or transmitted, in any form or by any means, electronic, mechanical, photocopying, recording or otherwise, without the prior permission of the publisher.

This book is sold subject to the condition that it shall not, by way of trade or otherwise, be lent, re-sold, hired out or otherwise circulated without the publisher's prior consent in any form of binding or cover other than that in which it is published.

ISBN 0-9517012-2-3
A catalogue record for this book is available from the British Library.
Copyright 1992 by David McGillivray.
Published by sun tavern fields, PO Box 982, London E1 9EQ.
Typesetting, paste-up &c by Counter Productions, London.
Printed by H.Charlesworth & Co. Ltd., Huddersfield, Great Britain.

For J.P.

Acknowledgments

This book is an expanded and updated version of a series of articles written for the magazine *Cinema* in 1982. Alan Jones suggested I should write the series to Alan McKenzie, the editor of *Cinema*, who commissioned it. Nearly ten years later Anthony Blampied of Sun Tavern Fields rediscovered the articles and asked me if I would like to adapt them into a book. As well as writing the Foreword, Pamela Green also corrected inaccuracies in Chapter 2. David Flint helped me with the research for Chapter 5. Illustrations were supplied from the collections of Michael Armstrong, Mark Ashworth, Martin Coxhead, Electric Video (Adam Cole, Steve Hughes), Allen Eyles, Pamela Green, Alan Jones, Stanley Long, Harrison Marks, National Film Archive, Kim Newman, New Realm Entertainments (Paul Hennessey) and Norman J. Warren. My grateful thanks to all.

CONTENTS

Foreword *by Pamela Green*	7
Introduction	13
1 The Pioneers	19
2 The Legends	27
3 The Grafters	51
4 The Final Days	67
5 The Aftermath	83
Appendix	103
Index	133

Pamela Green as nature intended

Foreword

I greatly enjoyed reading David's well researched and entertaining account of sex films made in Britain. This is a branch of film-making that needs to be exposed - the indifferent, the bad and the all too often just plain boring. I started nude modelling at the age of seventeen, so this is very much my subject.

While the British film industry is brilliant at parochial comedy, drama and historical subjects, it has not so far produced one really good film featuring the nude. The naturist films were, in the main, made by people with very little imagination for titillating the raincoat brigade, in the hope of making a few bob at the end of it all.

The girls were self-conscious and had little or no acting ability (compare them with Bardot and the films in which she appeared nude), and the directors, when confronted with the nude body, seemed to be totally unable to deal with it. There is a lot more that can be done other than throwing balls about. The locations, mostly sun clubs, were grotty and unsuitable, although it was the B.B.F.C.'s ruling that naturist films be set here.

In *Naked As Nature Intended*, which was filmed mainly in Cornwall (in fact the working title was *Cornish Holiday*), we never stopped running long enough to enjoy the locale. We always seemed to be waving, laughing (apparently at very little) and endlessly throwing beach balls. In the sequence shot at the Spielplatz sun club we were constricted by the lack of scenery: wooden huts, a small pool, a tennis court and a few trees do not readily lend themselves to people who want to paint with light, although Roy Poynter, the lighting cameraman, did an extraordinarily good job of the whole film, especially the last sequence of me in a hammock.

Charles Macaskie, who ran Spielplatz with his wife, was elderly and frail and lived in a heated caravan, so shots of him were understandably limited. Mrs Macaskie was made of sterner stuff, and was always out and about. Our male actor plodded about in walking shoes with the ubiquitous towel draped over one arm to cover the "dangly bits"; unfortunately he had a tendency to forget this and drop the towel. On publicity shots there he was, the offending "bits" in full view.

Now, apart from being a model, I was (and still am) a print finisher and re-toucher. Seven years at art school drawing nudes, and three years studying anatomy, had qualified me for this somewhat tedious work. I re-touched and finished every print that left our studios, including all the photographs for our *Kamera* magazine, so I had the unenviable task of making him fit for publication. Fortunately he was standing behind a fence, so I drew a climbing rose across the wire and incorporated the offending bits in with the leaves.

I would like to have made one well photographed, well scripted film featuring the nude body. The nearest I came to this was in 1960 in Michael Powell's classic *Peeping Tom*. In one scene with Carl Boehm I was totally nude, beautifully lit by Otto Heller. The re-cut version left just a glimpse of me at the far end of the bed. The first version was shown at the première and after that it was only seen overseas, although it has been known to surface in cinemas around London. The second is the one now shown on television.

On the subject of nudity and television: in these enlightened days, when virtually anything is shown, it seems incredible that an incident in 1964 caused such a furore. The Rediffusion programme *This Week* ran a feature on the glamour film scene and borrowed, among other material, one of mine called *The Window Dresser*. I watched the programme and was surprised that they showed a shot of me completely nude.

The following day most of the papers ran the story, and one viewer wrote to the radio programme *Woman's Hour* to express her horror and disgust: she practically accused me of blighting the lives of her children. (I'm not sure what the effect was on her husband - she didn't say). I wrote in reply, stating among many things that there was an OFF switch on her television. *Woman's Hour* was highly amused by all this and issued a challenge for the two of us to meet and make our points in an interview.

I duly arrived at Broadcasting House and was met by Molly Lee in the very grand entrance hall; from there we went into the bowels of the BBC, along many corridors, until we reached the recording studio, somewhere under Portland Place. The lady didn't show up, so Molly told me that I could continue on my own. I talked for fifteen minutes about my views on censorship and nudity, finishing with a quote from the Bible that "they were naked and not ashamed". I said that what was good enough for God was good enough for me. They broadcast the whole interview and have since repeated it many times.

Photographically, the scene at that time was very different from today. One had to observe the censorship laws on the removal of pubic hair, unless the pictures were sent to German magazines where it was considered indecent to be without it! Many commercial studios used nudes for their company calendars as well as product shots for their customers, and I was lucky enough to be used by most of them.

I even did a session for *Vogue* in 1954. Granted it was for a slimming and beauty article, but nevertheless I was nude. Even so, they were taking no chances. I was never alone with their photographer; there was always a *Vogue* lady present (presumably as a chaperone). To get one shot the photographer had to stand on the edge of the bath, but slipped and fell in. This caused great

COMPTON-CAMEO FILMS LTD.
60-62 Old Compton Street, London, W.1.   GER 1522 (5 lines)

PAMELA GREEN — *Lovely Star of "Naked - as Nature Intended"*

TASTE OF LOVE	LOLA	PAVEMENTS OF PARIS
THE CAPTIVE	THE TENEMENT	DAMNED AND THE DARING
ADVENTURES OF REMI	PARIS PLAYGIRLS	THE CALL GIRL BUSINESS
ASSASSINS IN THE SUN	FIRES ON THE PLAIN	LAST YEAR AT MARIENBAD

GHOST OF DRAG STRIP HOLLOW — MISSILE TO THE MOON

COUNT ON COMPTON-CAMEO FOR 1962

December (1961)
Sun	- 3 10 17 24 31
Mon	- 4 11 18 25
Tue	- 5 12 19 26
Wed	- 6 13 20 27
Thu	- 7 14 21 28
Fri	1 8 15 22 29
Sat	2 9 16 23 30

JANUARY 1962
SUN	MON	TUE	WED	THU	FRI	SAT
-	1	2	3	4	5	6
7	8	9	10	11	12	13
14	15	16	17	18	19	20
21	22	23	24	25	26	27
28	29	30	31	-	-	-

February (1962)
Sun	- 4 11 18 25
Mon	- 5 12 19 26
Tue	- 6 13 20 27
Wed	- 7 14 21 28
Thu	1 8 15 22
Fri	2 9 16 23
Sat	3 10 17 24

Naked As Nature Intended: Harrison Marks in the studio sand with (clockwise from top) Jackie Salt, Bridget Leonard, Angela Jones, Pamela Green, Petrina Forsyth

consternation and banging on doors, as for this shot my chaperone had been left outside because of a very confined working space. How a fully clad, sopping wet photographer clutching a large camera could have compromised me, we were both at a loss to understand.

Good figure models were in demand, and I worked for many studios and photographers. Magazines featuring nudes sold well and many, such as *Lilliput, London Opinion* and *Men Only*, always had one or two. This was in the days when *Men Only* was a pocket-size magazine featuring different photographers and writers, and not the publication it is today. Also, of course, there was *Health and Efficiency* and *Sun and Health*.

The famous trio of photographers - Walter Bird, John Everard and Roye - had been publishing books of nudes for years: my father had managed to obtain a copy of their *Eves Without Leaves* during the war. They, and many others, exhibited at the London Salon and the Royal Photographic Society annual exhibitions, and prints could always be purchased from the photographers.

When our Kamera Publications began in 1957, the sale of photographs from these and subsequent books we produced was our studio's main source of income. For all these different pictures it was essential to have a wardrobe of costumes and props, and in the Fifties the choice was endless. Weiss in Shaftesbury Avenue had a range of costumes and lingerie that is unobtainable today, and by 1958, when the 8mm glamour films began, it became even more essential to have a variety of costume. I ran an extensive wardrobe for myself and the models that we employed. I was using the same things in the Seventies and still have them today.

We have all come a long way since those early films and photographs, and at least in the Seventies I could model with much greater freedom. The history of the nude in all its diversity is a fascinating subject, and I collect books on this genre.

I look forward to adding *Doing Rude Things* to my collection.

Pamela Green
Isle of Wight
1992

Nudist Paradise: the first

Emmanuelle in Soho: the last

12

Introduction

I am that very rare animal, someone who has worked in the film business for more than six months without writing a book about it. Two things have stopped me putting pen to paper until now. Firstly I have never seen the appeal in writing about something that has already been written about by someone else. Being an inquisitive type, I prefer making discoveries rather than paraphrasing another writer's research.

Secondly I prefer a subject with a beginning, a middle and, most importantly, an end. The risk a writer takes, when dealing with a contemporary issue, is that it will reach its most significant development the day after his book is published, thus rendering it instantly worthless.

The options open to me, therefore, were limited in the extreme.

Skulking in my sub-conscious, however, was the topic with which destiny had paired me, the British sex film industry. Because it apparently had produced nothing of the slightest importance or interest, it was entirely undocumented. And here was a genre whose birth - with the production of Britain's first "nudie", *Nudist Paradise*, in 1957 - and death - with the release of her last soft porn comedy, *Emmanuelle in Soho*, in 1981 - were clearly demarcated.

At this juncture let us define the term "sex film". Throughout Continental Europe, the USA and Australia, and in some parts of Asia, it implies hard core pornography, openly available, although not necessarily consistently, since the early Seventies and, in some territories, the late Sixties. But pornography of this nature is certainly not within the field of this book, since the public presentation of unsimulated sex, whether live or recorded by any means, has always been illegal in Great Britain and the Republic of Ireland.

Because sexuality was barely acknowledged as a component part of the British temperament, it was inconceivable as the subject of commercial exploitation, and contraventions of the law were therefore few and far between for well over half the twentieth century.

Virtually all the blue movies shown at stag parties in Britain were smuggled into the country. Only one or two examples produced in Britain before World War II are known to exist. Regular production by amateurs was established in the late Forties, but it was not until the Sixties that a handful of professionals appeared on the scene.

The only British pornographers to be known by name were Evan Phillips, Michael Freeman and John Lindsay. Evan Phillips, dubbed "Britain's first blue millionaire", made short films on 8mm ("loops") in London from 1965. After serving an eighteen month prison sentence for possessing obscene materials, he committed suicide in 1975 at the age of 33.

Michael Freeman, also at work in London from the mid-Sixties, had been imprisoned twice by the end of the decade. He was back in business in 1980, when he began directing hard core porn on videotape, which he thought would be outside the scope of the 1959 Obscene Publications Act. He was mistaken. In 1982 he was imprisoned yet again.

John Lindsay switched from photography (he was stills cameraman on Derek Ford's *The Wife Swappers* in 1969) to pornography in the late Sixties and was for many years the industry's most eloquent advocate. He was acquitted of conspiring to publish obscene films at Birmingham Crown Court in 1975, but jailed in London in 1983 for exhibiting them.

Hard core porn, including *Deep Throat* and many other famous titles, was screened at cinema clubs in most of Britain's major cities for a decade (1975-1986). Freeman's "adult" videotapes were openly advertised in magazines at the turn of the Eighties. Since then, hard core videotapes, both straight and gay, have surfaced occasionally, but are not common.

The soft core sex film, in which there may be partial or complete nudity and, in later films, simulated sex, has existed throughout the world since the Fifties. The genre, which aimed to tease and titillate, was rendered pretty well obsolete in the Seventies by that which showed everything in unflinching close-up. But, for something like ten years, while the two types of movie co-existed, the soft core sex film was programmed by every British cinema save the snootiest art-house, and became more familiar to cinemagoers than the musical and the Western.

At the top end of the market, some films were sufficiently well-made to acquire a measure of respectability - Denmark's *Seventeen* (1965), the American/West German co-production *Thérèse and Isabelle* (1968), Hong Kong's *Intimate Confessions of a Chinese Courtesan* (1973), Holland's *Turkish Delight* (1973), France's *Emmanuelle* (1974) and *Bilitis* (1976), and Brazil's *Dona Flor and Her Two Husbands* (1976).

The majority of the more lowbrow offerings were imported from West Germany, France and Italy. French directors Max Pécas and Jean Rollin developed their followings. Actresses such as Terry Torday, Sybill Danning and Claudine Beccarie became well-known to regular punters.

From farther afield, two Australian sex comedies - *Stork* (1971) and *Alvin Purple* (1973) - made a splash. The bulk of America's enormous sexploitation output was never shown publically in Britain although some of the work of Russ Meyer, Joe Sarno and others later gained a cult reputation in repertory cinemas.

Of the American films that reached a wider audience in Britain, those that made a lasting impression included *Deadly Weapons* (1974), which exhibited the 73" bust of Chesty Morgan; *Flesh Gordon* (1974), an expensive sci-fi sex comedy complete with stop-motion monsters; *The Happy Hooker* (1975), a heavily bowdlerised biopic of Dutch-born brothel madame Xaviera Hollander; and *Linda Lovelace for President* (1975), in which Hollywood's most famous porn queen could at least be seen simulating the skill that made her a star.

In darkest Britain, the only form of sexual entertainment generally available has been of the soft core variety, but for nearly 25 years it just about drove the populace to distraction. While a minority of moralists cursed the sex film as the harbinger of a tidal wave of filth, the majority of the male population and a good percentage of curious females turned it into the most lucrative speculation the British film industry has ever enjoyed.

It is improbable that Britain will ever find a more profitable genre of film and, although the sex film seems to count for nothing in the scheme of things, the last and most devastating downswing in British film production coincided with the cessation of the sex film business at the end of the Seventies.

No matter what yardstick one uses - even, for example, low budget production in general - sex films, particularly the British ones, were extremely poor. They were characterised by inane writing, hack direction, amateurish performances, technical inadequacy and a consequent deficiency of entertainment value. Even one or two films that were at least competently made, e.g. *Cool It Carol!* (1970), *Exposé* (1975) and *The Stud* (1978), were dismissed by critics as rubbish.

To understand why the films were so popular, one need look no further than *No Sex Please - We're British*, the longest-running comedy in the history of the British theatre, which kept coachloads of day trippers in hysterics for more than sixteen years (1971-1987).

The implication of the title is that the British, nursing their stiff upper lips and hot water bottles in ardour-dampening rain, don't have sex, a joke probably appreciated the world over. Apparently the play has been successfully produced abroad; but it is inconceivable that its action could be relocated to any other country. *No Sex Please - We're French* is patently absurd. But then so is *No Sex Please - We're Bulgarian*. And indeed *American*.

The play's title is actually a fair summation of its inimitably British plot: an ordinary young couple is mistakenly sent consignments of dirty postcards, books and films, and goes berserk trying to conceal them from stock figures of authority (policeman, bank manager, mother-in-law).

The Great British public, unaccustomed to the nudity and sexual candour taken more for granted by other nations, seemed to go similarly barmy from 1957 to 1981, running from film to film, regardless of their quality and their content and even how much material had been removed by the censor.

Although some major studios, notably Columbia and EMI, were later persuaded to invest in sex films, most of the product emanated from tightly-budgeted, independent companies based in Wardour Street and its surrounding alleys in the heart of London's seedy Soho district.

As in other countries, the sex film took many forms, beginning with the naturist pictures of the Fifties and developing into sex drama, sex education, sex documentary and sex fantasy. But the staple diet of the British industry was sex comedy, usually tailor-made for its repressed audience (and ever-vigilant censor) by severely limiting the actual sexual contact.

Foreigners may have fallen about at the sight of the Act in mid-consummation, but the ideal scenario for a British sex comedy was to have its lovebirds surprised by a third party while sex was still a concept. The woman would pull the sheet up to her neck, and the man would be caught with his trousers down, revealing nothing as vulgar as genitals but, typically, shirt-tails and red spotted shorts.

If it seems extraordinary that anyone should want to write about sex films that were not only badly made but also, as often as not, unsexy, I can only submit that it is this very contradiction that fascinates me, just as horror films that are not frightening and melodramas that are not exciting are now inspiring other books.

So many other books, in fact, that they are beginning to compete for space on the shelves with books about films that are works of art or merely worth seeing. But the appeal of the good film is obvious. It is the bad film which reveals the far more intriguing motives of the people who chose to make it and the people who chose to watch it.

Why it has taken me so long to bow to fate and squeeze the lowly sex film into its historical niche I cannot imagine. From childhood I have been strangely attracted by the second-rate and the downright worthless, regularly cold-shouldering the box-office success that will live forever in favour of the flop that may never be seen again.

I am also uniquely qualified as far as this particular subject is concerned, having seen, either as a paying customer or a critic, most of the films described, and met and/or worked with most of the people who made them. Because I wanted this first and, more than likely, only history of the British sex film to be an overall view, not a personal memoir, I deliberately have not mentioned my involvement in certain films. But for the sake of the accuracy I hope I have maintained throughout, I have come as clean as possible under the circumstances in the appendix.

Another one in the can: Stanley Long (right) photographs *A Promise of Bed*

The enduring image: Anita Love in *Nudist Paradise*

Carl Conway on the brink of *Nudist Paradise*

Chapter 1: "The Pioneers"

When they write their monographs on the Cinema of the Twentieth Century, what will historians make of the two and a half decades that produced the British sex film? Not a jot. Utterly worthless and insignificant, the genre will be completely ignored.

Nor is it likely that middle-class intellectuals will rediscover the films in order to laugh at them at late night screenings. Unlike such chic trash as *Plan 9 From Outer Space* and *Santa Claus Conquers the Martians*, British sex films lack even the redeeming quality of being so bad they're good. They're simply unwatchable by any standards, and will consequently disappear without trace, leaving future generations to wonder, "What were they like?"

Evidence of the films is already disappearing. Distributors have destroyed the publicity material. In some cases the films themselves have vanished: archives weren't interested in preserving them, and, whereas even Edgar Lustgarten's *Scotland Yard Mysteries* - generally regarded as the lowest of the low - turned up on television, the British sex film had virtually no re-sale value whatever. The most important links of all are also breaking: Robert Hartford-Davis, Antony Balch, Mary Millington, and many others who created the films, are dead.

This book was written not only to record the fact that the era of the British sex film did indeed exist, but also to propose that it should not have been swept under the carpet without as much as a second thought.

This is not because the films are worthy of closer critical attention. Other countries may have produced classics of movie erotica; Britain hasn't. But as pointers to the obsessions and hypocrisies of an age which influenced many of the film-makers at work today, these films have at last acquired true value.

They were nothing short of a social phenomenon. At a time when most British films found it difficult to recoup their production costs from world sales, sex films made their money back from the home market alone. What made the British public flock to see such rubbish? And why are the titles of these films - *Take Off Your Clothes and Live, Naked as Nature Intended, Can You Keep It Up For a Week?* - still common parlance?

The breeding ground for the sex film was post-war Britain, its male population eager for the more titillating entertainments they'd seen while on active service abroad. In 1951 the British Board of Film Censors bowed to the inevitable and introduced the "X" certificate, which allowed the exhibition of films that previously would have been cut or banned outright.

By the mid-Fifties many of Britain's major cities were able to support cinemas whose staple diet was the Continental "X" film. Most of this product came from France, Italy and Sweden and consisted of sleazy melodramas with titles like *Forbidden Women* and *The Fruits of Summer*, their plots usually revolving around prostitution or vice rings.

Today's censorship may appear to be tightening, but it is a model of enlightenment compared to the dark days of the Fifties. The film of Jean-Paul Sartre's play *The Respectable Prostitute* was shown as *La P... Respectueuse*, and the story is told that, after viewing a French film with bedroom scenes, octogenarian censor Sir Sidney Harris remarked, "I suppose we shall have to pass it, but men and women don't go to bed together with no clothes on."

The thrill of discovering something the censor had let slip through must have been intoxicating. Stanley Long, Britain's leading sex film producer throughout the Sixties and Seventies, told me, "I remember that in 1956 I travelled over to the other side of London to see a subtitled French film that was reputed to have a nipple showing."

Britain's first attempt at a sleazy melodrama on the Continental model was *The Flesh Is Weak* in 1957. It was unrepresentative of the British sex film as it later developed in that it was a product of the studio system and featured a Hollywood star, John Derek (whose future wife, Bo, was at this time one year old), in the leading role as a Soho pimp.

But its treatment of pre-Wolfenden street vice - three parts sensationalism, one part social concern - qualifies it as Britain's first modern sexploitation film, and its makers - producer Raymond Stross and director Don Chaffey - were clearly aware of what they were doing: a year later they put out *A Question of Adultery* with its even more daring theme of artificial insemination.

These films, however, broke no new censorship barriers; but a film that did arrived in Britain at this period. It led to the most substantial relaxation of film censorship since its institution in 1913, and in so doing was directly responsible for the establishment of the British sex film industry. Yet, ironically enough, it had a "U" certificate and no sex. It was *The Garden of Eden*, an American naturist picture made in 1954.

Acting on its precept that the naked breasts of white women were not permissible, the B.B.F.C. banned the film. Undeterred, its distributor took it to the London County Council, which found nothing to object to. Indeed, not only was the film scrupulously unerotic, it also had worthy credentials, being sponsored by the American Sunbathing Association, and photographed in colour by the great Polish cameraman Boris Kaufman, who had lit the French masterpieces *Zéro de conduite* and *L'Atalante*.

These considerations did not, of course, concern the British public, who quite simply had never seen naked breasts and buttocks on the screen before - apart, that is, from a glimpse of the nude bathing in the Swedish film *One Summer of Happiness* in 1952. (The famous nude shots of Hedy Lamarr in the

The evils of Soho: John Derek threatens Patricia Jessel in *The Flesh Is Weak*

The Reluctant Nudist: the end of innocence

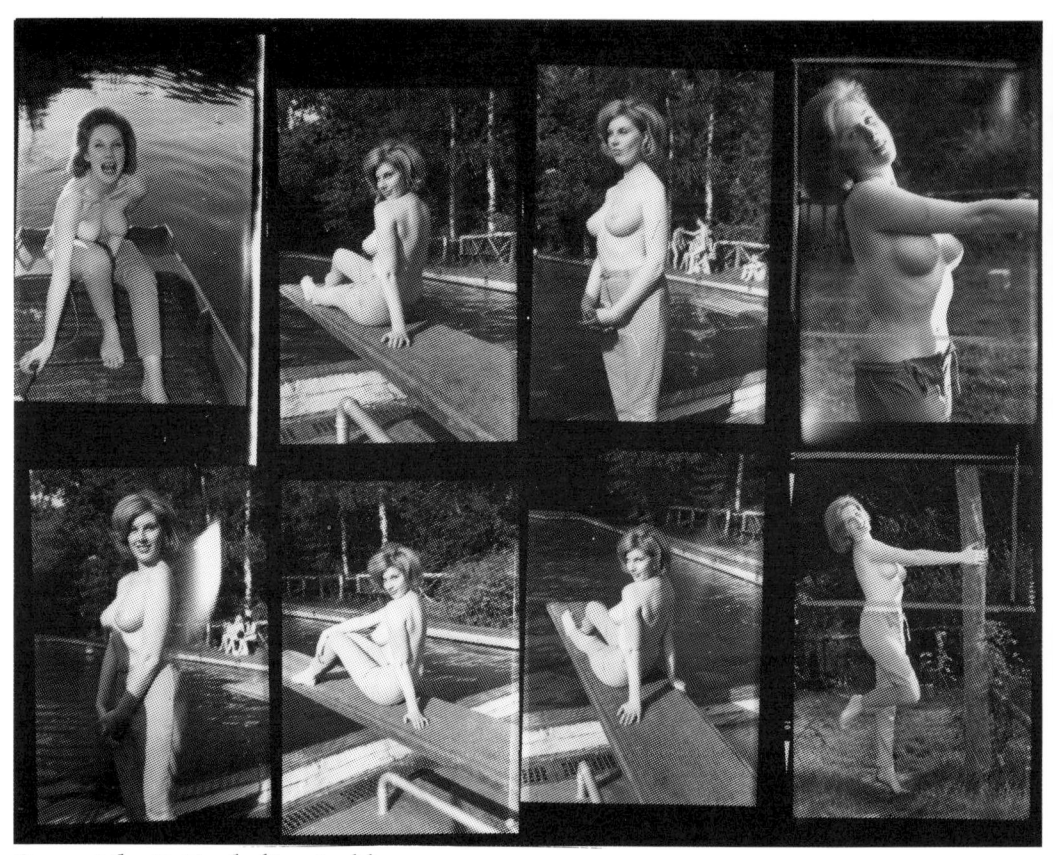

Some Like It Cool: directed by a very pompous young man

1933 Czech film *Ecstasy* were completely removed for British release.)

A clamour began for more nudist films, but only the more recondite could be obtained: two American productions made in the Thirties and a Mexican production of *Adam and Eve*. Consequently, in 1958, Britain produced her first "nudie", *Nudist Paradise*, in the full glory of Eastman Colour and Nudiscope.

Little enough is known about these pioneering days of the sex film business, but one fact totally forgotten is that the man who brought *The Garden of Eden* to Britain, and the man who produced the trail-blazing *Nudist Paradise*, were one and the same. He was Nat Miller, who laboured down the bottom end of the British film industry for sixty years and was still at it when he was well into his seventies.

In the business virtually from the day he left school, aged 15, in 1924, Miller spent thirty years as a backroom boy with the firm that grew into the Granada empire. He left in December, 1954, and, by the following May, he'd already produced two films. One of them, *It's a Great Day*, scored him another first: never before had a film been based on a TV series, in this case the popular soap opera *The Grove Family*.

When I first met him in 1982, Miller was reticent about discussing the reasons he had for associating himself with films featuring naked actors, a brave and risky venture in 1957. "The point about show business is this," he offered, "and this has been my experience for so many years: give the public something they've never seen before and you've got a market."

Miller shot part of *Nudist Paradise* during the Naturist World Congress held at the publicity-conscious Duke of Bedford's stately home Woburn Abbey. Directed by Charles Saunders, brother of *Mousetrap* producer, Peter, it starred former dancer Katy Cashfield, who went on to appear in a few more glamour girl roles, and American actor Carl Conway, who later became a voice-over artist.

Despite the fact that, as Miller put it, "There were no full... er... frontals or anything like that at all", the actresses had to conform to contemporary moral standards by shaving their pubic hair.

Both Miller and his cast maintained that stripping naked entailed no embarrassment. Said Conway, "I guess I was just like any novice nudist when I first got to Spielplatz [the St Albans naturist reserve where most British nudies were filmed]. But I don't need to tell you just how easy it is to get accustomed to naturism. And after the first uneasy few minutes, it all seemed so completely natural. I enjoyed making this film tremendously. It was just like a holiday." (This lack of inhibition was not confirmed by others I interviewed.)

Nudist Paradise was reviewed only by the trade press, one of whose critics called it "trite and stupid." Even the nudists' monthly *The Naturist* was forced to concede that the acting was "of only average competence, which is never helped by the peculiarly insipid dialogue."

Financial success, however, was a cast-iron certainty. Costing only £15,000, two thirds of which was invested by American producers Milton Subotsky and Max J. Rosenberg (later to form Amicus, a spirited rival to Hammer Films), *Nudist Paradise* grossed £19,000 from its British release alone, and was the most profitable Miller ever made. Strangely there was no follow-up. "I got too deeply involved in other productions," he explained somewhat vaguely.

In the early Sixties Miller produced two sexploiters with taboo-breaking themes: *That Kind of Girl* (1961) was about venereal disease; *The Yellow Teddybears* (1963) concerned schoolgirl sex.

Miller then returned to distribution, but, at the turn of the Seventies, when the dwindling number of cinemas made the continuation of his one-man operation impossible, he gave up, and ended his career selling films to TV and video companies. When I last saw him, he was working from a dingy office with a rattling fan heater, and was trying to move out of his suburban London flat because he couldn't afford the rent.

Others made millions from sex films, but not Nat Miller, the man who started it all. "Sad it may be, but that's life," he smiled. At that time *Nudist Paradise* was still playing to naturists in Australia. Perhaps it still is.

When *The Garden of Eden* was passed by 180 of the 230 local authorities to which Miller submitted it, the B.B.F.C. backed down and decided to award certificates (usually an "A", which required children under the age of sixteen to be accompanied by an adult) to nudist films. The provisos were that pubic hair and genitals must not be visible, and that settings must be recognisable as nudist camps.

In *What the Censor Saw*, the revealing autobiography of John Trevelyan, a censor from 1951 and Secretary of the B.B.F.C. from 1958 to 1971, Trevelyan writes, "Normally the more genuine the film the more problems it gave us; when real nudist gatherings were filmed we carefully removed all sight of genitals, if necessary going through the film several times to make sure we had not missed any."

The success of *Nudist Paradise* provoked an outbreak of screen stripping that was almost indecent. The Danziger Brothers, expatriate Americans who, up until this time, had been quite content to mass produce second-features, rushed out *The Nudist Story* (1959), the first nudie to involve an established actor (Anthony Oliver).

An ambitious young director named Michael Winner came up with *Some Like It Cool* (1960), often cited today - with Winner's jovial agreement - as an example of how bad the nudie could be.

The films of genuine naturist Michael Keatering, some featuring "the fabulous sub-aqua star" Yannick (a famous nude celebrity of the era), managed to bend the censors' rules still further: in *Sunswept* (1961) actors

Because they couldn't wear golliwogs

were seen naked, not only in the nudist colony, but also on a yacht *on their way to the nudist colony.* "We decided that it would be inequitable to refuse it a certificate," said Trevelyan.

The rituals of the nudie became well-known and much parodied in the press and on TV. Ninety per cent of the plots were identical: a person in some way hostile to the naturists' cause would be talked, or tricked, into visiting a colony. Then, after watching displays of trampolining or volleyball, the opponent would delightedly remove his or her own clothes.

Any physical contact between the nudists was expressly forbidden, and the dreaded genitals were hidden either behind towels or conveniently placed shrubs.

The sight of these semi-clad people, virtually all of whom were attractive young girls, titillated an audience that was virtually all male. There cannot have been one sane adult in the country who believed these films were being made for the delectation of the sun worshipper, yet producers had to maintain this pretense at all costs for fear of being refused a certificate. Stanley Long summed up the extraordinary paradox that distinguished early British sexploitation:

"It was absolutely taboo to imply anything to do with sex. Everybody had to appear to be uninterested in sex in any shape or form. It was totally the health kick and jolly hockey sticks and volleyball. Volleyball was always a great favourite because it used to make the tits bounce up and down."

This ridiculous situation was to be short-lived. It is a very small step from the purity of nudity to the inescapable sexuality of striptease. This step was about to be taken and, once it had been allowed by the censors, there was to be no turning back.

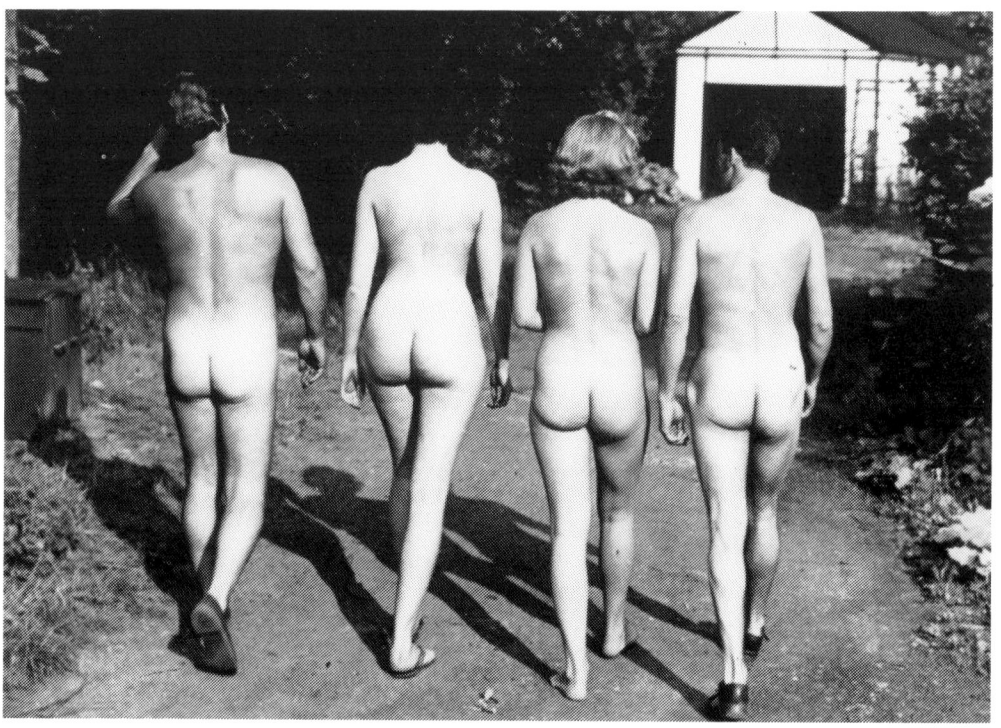

Nudist Paradise: completely natural

Chapter 2: "The Legends"

Britain was goaded into making her own sex films by the precedents set by America and the rest of Europe. But it was a subject she should have left well alone.

Whereas her sophistication in the drawing room was unquestioned, her naïveté in the bedroom was world-renowned. Sixty years of Victorian repression had bequeathed the British a further fifty of timidity and guilt during which time sex was seldom publically referred to except in the music-hall and on seaside postcards. These institutions had firmly established in British minds the sex act as naughty, or dirty, or sometimes both, but never erotic. It had also become inextricably associated with the lavatory.

Inevitably these prejudices were a salient feature of what was to become a thriving British industry - the production of sex comedies. The first full-fledged British sex comedy was *Mary Had a Little* (1961), which paired saucy French Agnès Laurent with English silly ass Jack Watling; it was the last movie to be made by Marx Brothers director Edward Buzzell.

But the films which were to propagate Sex-English Style to curious audiences throughout the world were those in the *Carry On* series. The first, *Carry On Sergeant* (1958), was a National Service farce with little sexual innuendo, but when the famous daffodil joke in the follow-up, *Carry On Nurse* (1959), caused little short of a national sensation, producer Peter Rogers saw the light. Subsequent films became increasingly risqué, and in *Carry on Regardless* (1961) the puns were, for their time, extremely rude. (Example: Charles Hawtrey has mistaken a strip club for an aviary. Manager: "What do you want?" Hawtrey: "Your birds. Oh, I can't wait! Tell me - what sort are they?" Manager: "What sort do you like?" Hawtrey: "Blue tits." Manager: "Eh?" Hawtrey: "Got any?" Manager: "No. My place is centrally heated.")

Most of the 31 *Carry On* films, particularly those later in the series, were strained and unfunny, but two - *Carry On Cleo* (1964) and *Carry On Cowboy* (1965) - were inventively witty and are among the handful of British sex comedies that are actually worth seeing. (The others are Pete Walker's *Cool It Carol!* [1970] and *The Four Dimensions of Greta* [1972] and Martin Campbell's *Eskimo Nell* [1974]).

Given the prominence of the variety theatre in the growth of prurience in Britain, it is hardly surprising that many of the leading figures of the British sexploitation business had music-hall backgrounds.

Arnold Louis Miller is the nephew of Nat Mills, half of the knockabout comedy act Nat Mills and Bobby, which played the London Palladium and several Royal Command performances. Two sex film makers, Harrison Marks and Pete Walker, began their careers as stand-up comics. And although

No sex, please - we're British: Sidney James in *Carry On Regardless*

The men behind *Nudes of the World:* production manager Harry Green, director Arnold Louis Miller, cameraman Stanley Long, actor Colin Goddard, executive producer Philip Kutner

Stanley Long originally had no music-hall ties, he eventually succumbed to its strange allure and, like Marks and Walker, packed his films with veteran farceurs.

The most open and perennially adolescent of Britain's former sex movie supremos, Stanley Long, a working-class Londoner born in 1933, started out, like two of his more illustrious colleagues, Russ Meyer and Just Jaeckin, as a photographer. In the late Forties he was an apprentice at one of the London fashion studios where the celebrated Barbara Goalen posed, and in the early Fifties he was an assistant to the society photographer Maurice Ambler, whose work was familiar to the readers of *The Strand Magazine* and *Picture Post*, both now defunct.

Liberated from his two years' compulsory National Service (he was a medical orderly for the R.A.F.), Long, like many fellow conscripts, determined to set up his own business. But he was only scraping a living photographing weddings and catalogue merchandise until he was introduced to the expanding sex business by a 15-year-old schoolgirl. Her name was Hilary Donaldson and when, in 1955, she became the youngest girl ever to be hired as a dancer for London's cheeky Windmill theatre, where showgirls posed in nude tableaux, Long took her photo for the *Weekend Mail*.

Hilary's career as a Windmill girl was short-lived. A year later she had become a switchboard operator for a paper manufacturers but, as chance would have it, they were planning to branch out into the publication of "art studies" (a Fifties euphemism for photographs of naked women) and wanted Hilary to model for them.

She in turn recommended Long to take the pictures. "That'll be fun," he said to himself. "I've never photographed a naked lady before," and with that he was lost to wedding portraiture forever. Soon he had his own studio, where a new breed of working girl would sit, naked but demure, before hurrying off to repeat the process for Long's rivals Russell Gay and Harrison Marks.

Some of the resulting art studies appeared in a girlie mag called *Photo Studio*, published by L. Miller and Son, a company whose more respectable operations included importing from the U.S.A. Marvel comics. L. Miller's son was Arnold Louis Miller, who, in 1958, was a 36-year-old businessman with every prospect of remaining one. But when Long told him he had begun making litle movies of his models removing their clothes, Miller, who had no particular interest in films but a shrewd business sense, suggested that the Long productions could be advertised in *Photo Studio* and sold by mail order.

These were the first of Britain's so-called "glamour films", the prettily-packaged 8mm striptease shorts that proliferated until the mid-Sixties. Each featuring a girl who took approximately two and a half minutes to strip to her panties, the films were almost wholesome in their lack of obscenity, but this did not prevent laboratories refusing to process them, or moral groups of the

Entente cordiale: Jack Watling and Agnès Laurent in *Mary Had a Little*

The Reluctant Nudist: indecent but for the air-brush

Stag Films: a thousand prints a day

A scene cut from *Naked As Nature Intended:* John Trevelyan said "No, no, no, no, no"

day expressing their disgust as the little boxes began to turn up in the corner newsagent.

They were very big business indeed. Long made nearly a hundred of the movies, and Stag Films, the company he formed with Miller, was at one time despatching a thousand prints a day.

But in 1959 the partners found bigger fish to fry. *Nudist Paradise*, the first British nudist feature film, had been coining money, and it inspired Long and Miller to make their own nudie, *Nudist Memories*, which was shot in a week "in absolute ignorance" at Spielplatz.

In the film, one of the girls who visits the St Albans naturist reserve was played by a young stripper named Anna Karen; a decade later she was to find fame as the fat and bespectacled Olive in TV's *On the Buses*.

Deciding, having cut it together, that *Nudist Memories* was by dint of its naked breasts saleable, its makers gave it a Hammond organ soundtrack and showed it to veteran distributor, E.J. Fancey. Present at the screening was "a very pompous young man" named Michael Winner, who at that time had already directed several second-features for Fancey. Long likes to think it was his film that encouraged Winner to make his own nudie, *Some Like It Cool*.

E.J. Fancey agreed to distribute *Nudist Memories*. Cock-a-hoop, Long went round snapping the cinemas where it was showing. "If my memory serves me correctly," he pondered, 23 years after the event, "the budget for *Nudist Memories* was a thousand pounds...or was it seven hundred?"

Director Miller and cameraman Long went on to make another nine features together. The next was the documentary exposé *West End Jungle* (1961), made for £3,200 on a borrowed camera. It claimed to prove how the Street Offences Act of 1960 had succeeded only in concealing London's vice and corruption underground. In fact all the incidents in the film - scenes in clip joints and phoney massage parlours and photographic studios - were staged. The prostitutes were in reality au pairs recruited from a coffee bar in Soho's Dean Street, and their clients were played by friends of the crew.

Despite this the film was widely praised for its authenticity; and when it was refused a certificate by both the B.B.F.C. and the London County Council, its distributor organised an outcry. "Is London ashamed of itself?" demanded the *News of the World*. "It should be generally released," said the Reverend Donald Soper. "I sincerely hope there will be second thoughts," added Labour peer Lord Stonham.

The film's supporters were of course unaware that this indictment of London's vice and corruption was made by those who, only two years earlier, could have been accused of contributing to it. As it turned out, however, the protests were to no avail. The film is without a censor's certificate to this day.

Forsaking social documentary, Long and Miller returned to the more profitable area of naked breasts and buttocks, producing *Nudes of the World*

West End Jungle: Nothing is real

(1961) and the fabled *Take Off Your Clothes and Live* (1962). The first, narrated by Valerie Singleton, later renowned as one of the first presenters of the children's television series *Blue Peter*, was about thirteen beauty queens who open their own nudist camp, while the second concerned nine beautiful girls travelling to the French naturist paradise, the Isle de Levant. The extras were genuine naturists, ludicrously attired in G-strings, and the style of presentation was so gauche that today it looks like self-parody.

It was impossible, according to Long, to find actors willing to strip, and therefore most of the casts came from model agencies. "We foolishly thought we could turn them into actors in a fortnight," he admitted. "Of course they were totally wooden and stilted. It's amazing that we ever got away with it. But I guess that really people weren't looking at the acting. And I don't really know why we went to such lengths to incorporate dialogue in these films because people only went to see the spectacle of lots of naked girls."

A story Arnold Louis Miller tells about *Take Off Your Clothes and Live* says a great deal about his artistic criteria as a nudie director.

"I nearly had a stand-up fight with the second male lead. I had to have one shot - I think it was the sunset shot - and he took umbrage about it and he said he wasn't going to do it. And I said, 'Well, if you're not going to do it, I'm going to get rid of you.' And he said, 'You can't write me out of the picture at this stage.' I said, 'Oh yes I can. I'll just have one of the artists say "Where's Tom?" And the other bloke'll say, "Oh, he had to leave."' Half an hour later this actor said he'd do the shot."

Despite a budget which, at £14,000, was twice that of *Nudes of the World*, *Take Off Your Clothes and Live* did not fare as well at the box-office. And yet its title has lived on and is still coined today by pundits speaking disparagingly of the naturist ethos. Was it intended to be tongue-in-cheek in 1962?

Long: "Yeah, it was."

Really?

"All right, no, it wasn't. I'll tell you what it was. It was just a contrived title to excite the type of patron these films were aimed at. I mean, taking off your clothes is a bit naughty, and then... *live*... I mean, that suggests *Take Off Your Clothes and Fuck*. I suppose that was the thinking behind it: that it might imply sexual activity."

In 1964 Long and Miller were asked to make the first (and, as it turned out, the last) British travelogue in Circlorama, a Russian invention which involved the audience standing inside a 360° screen. A novelty during the London tourist season, it later flopped in Blackpool and Glasgow and was abandoned before the project had recovered its costs. But for Long it posed several enjoyable challenges, one of which is that cameras shooting a complete 360° angle will inevitably photograph the crew. (They eventually hid by crouching under the duralumin plate on which the eleven cameras were mounted.)

Mondo Cane, the Italian shockumentary which dwelled gloatingly on various aspects of man's savagery, spawned dozens of imitations during the Sixties, two of which - *London in the Raw* (1964) and *Primitive London* (1965) - were next out of the Long-Miller stable. In both these cases the reward for enduring the unpleasantries, which included a hair transplant operation and the killing of a battery chicken, was sex: striptease, a woman giving birth, and the reconstruction of a wife-swapping party (a subject to which Long was later to return.)

The inclusion of such hitherto forbidden material was the result of Sixties permissiveness breaking down the bounds of censorship. The graphic depiction of sexuality was still some years off, but the degree of liberation achieved in the mid-Sixties was apparent in the names of the films themselves.

In 1960 foreign sexploitation films were still being given English titles which reflected the British audience's guilty conscience: *Sins of Youth; Girl of Shame; Forgive Us Our Trespasses; Let's Be Daring, Madame*. But in 1964 the censors allowed an Italian film to be given the shamelessly open title *Sex Can Be Difficult*, and henceforward it was sex, and not vice, corruption and nudity, that sold the exploitation film.

It was in this enlightened atmosphere that Long and Miller produced their first unadulterated sex film, *Secrets of a Windmill Girl* (1965). Originally intended as a straightforward record of the last nude revue presented at the Windmill theatre, its cramped dance routines and comic fillers were later woven into a fictitious story concerning a detective's investigations into the death of a former Windmill girl.

Important as documentary evidence of the kind of tat that inflamed the senses of a million voyeurs during the three decades the Windmill operated non-stop revue, the film is also of interest in that it features early - clothed - appearances by singer-actress Dana Gillespie and Oscar nominee Pauline Collins.

Shortly after the film's release Stanley Long and Arnold Louis Miller went their separate ways. For Long the split was especially beneficial leading as it did to a range of work far exceeding the confines of low-budget exploitation. His most prestigious assignment - never publically revealed until now - was on Roman Polanski's first British film, *Repulsion*, in 1965.

Polanski, a perfectionist given to shooting ten minutes' footage on a five second cut-away of a clock, had fallen so far behind schedule that only two thirds of the film had been completed by the time his cameraman, Gilbert Taylor, was forced to leave to fulfil other obligations. Producer Michael Klinger invited Long to replace him; and after studying the rushes to duplicate Taylor's lighting, Long photographed, uncredited, the remainder of the film, which comprised all Catherine Deneuve's fantasies (including the descending ceiling), John Fraser's corpse in the bath, the cracked pavements, and several

Stanley Long and Arnold Louis Miller: implying sexual activity

scenes in the pub and the beauty parlour.

Both Long and Miller were involved in the two British horror films directed by doomed *wunderkind* Michael Reeves. Long photographed *The Sorcerers* (1967); this and *Witchfinder General* (1968) were co-produced by Miller. Sensationally brutal (and therefore heavily censored), the films were defended by some critics, who perceived, particularly in *Witchfinder*, a moral statement about the sickening futility of violence. This view, however, takes on a somewhat hollow tone when judged against Long's eyewitness account of Michael Reeves at work:

"He was flinging blood about on the set like it was going out of fashion, I mean gallons of it. I used to constantly be checking him. He had this obsessive thing about throwing it up the walls, and when Susan George was stabbed with a pair of scissors, it was going all over the cameras and all over the crew and everybody's clothes, and I said, 'Really, you know, come off it.' But he loved it. He seemed to revel in it. He definitely had a kink about blood."

Insecure and highly strung, Reeves was only 25 when he killed himself in 1969.

That year Long produced and photographed three sex films - *A Promise of Bed*, *Groupie Girl* and *The Wife Swappers* - directed by the writer Derek Ford, who was to become a prominent figure of the British sex cinema of the Seventies. *The Wife Swappers*, one of the most successful British sex films ever made, but condemned by even the *News of the World* critic as "one of the worst films I've ever seen", convinced Long that he was now capable of directing films himself.

For his first he chose a sex comedy. He had had no experience in directing comedy, and this was self-evident in the finished product, *Bread* (1971), a slow and witless piece about a group of hippies trying to organise a pop festival.

Returning to the quasi-documentary format with which he was familiar, Long directed *Naughty!* (1971), a history of pornography; *On the Game* (1973), a history of prostitution; and *It Could Happen to You* (1975), which, when it was first seen, purported to be a warning to adolescents about the perils of V.D. (Its probity was thrown into some doubt when it was re-issued a few months later as *Intimate Teenage Secrets*.)

By the mid-Seventies sex films were such a dependable proposition that the major studios moved in to cream off some of the profits. Most of the big business interlopers failed to get the tit-and-bum formula right, but Columbia's *Confessions* films, sex comedies designed as ruder versions of the *Carry On* films, were for a time just what the public wanted. They were themselves much imitated, the result being that, by the end of the Seventies, the market had been saturated and the *Carry On* series was discontinued until 1992.

Three of the *Confessions* rip-offs were directed by Stanley Long. He had

Strippers, sex, chickens...

Shirley Valentine was not Pauline Collins' first film

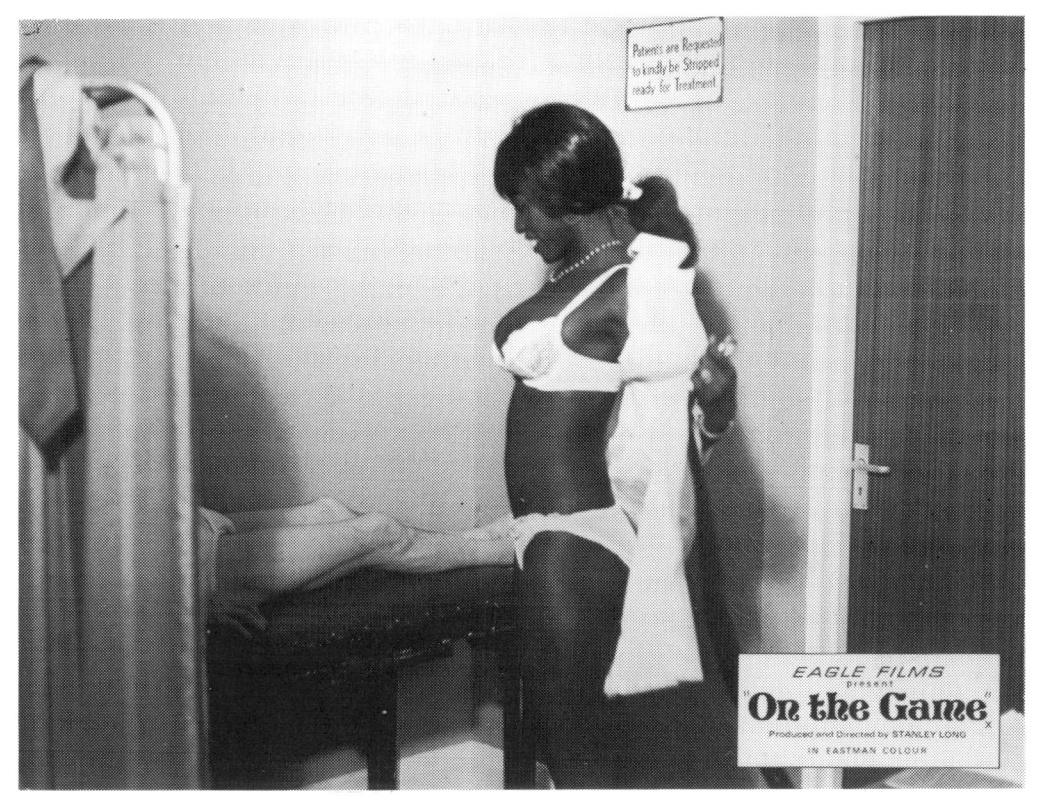

Sex therapy: Lucienne in *On the Game*

Elaine Paige was not amused

been hankering to return to comedy, and with *Adventures of a Taxi Driver* (1975), he did so with spectacular success. Made for less than £60,000 and grossing £400,000, it ended up among Britain's Top 20 box office champions for 1976.

This achievement may have been due partly to Long's more accomplished direction of such comedy stalwarts as Diana Dors, Liz Fraser, Ian Lavender and Stephen Lewis, but it is more specifically attributable to the personality of Barry Evans, who seemed to have just the right degree of timidity to play a British sex film hero.

Evans refused to sign for the sequel, *Adventures of a Private Eye* (1977), and despite the acquisition of another brigade of comic talent - Harry H. Corbett, Fred Emney, Irene Handl, Jon Pertwee, William Rushton - the film, although profitable, failed to equal the grosses of its predecessor. By 1978, when *Adventures of a Plumber's Mate* was released, the sex film boom was all but over, and, in an attempt to boost the takings, Long's company was reduced to publicising the fact that a supporting role was played by Elaine Paige, who had recently shot to stardom in the stage musical *Evita*. Miss Paige was not amused.

Blaming the abolition of government subsidy, the "unrealistic" wage demands of the technicians' unions, and the law of diminishing returns, Long quit full-time film production in 1978 and set up a distributor called Alpha Films. Well-connected, it released a number of crowd-pleasers, including *Rabid, The Kentucky Fried Movie* and *The Exterminator*, before selling out to Intervision in 1982. Intervision later became the company that now runs the Ritz chain of video stores.

Long's ex-partner, Arnold Louis Miller, took a very different path. Although he claimed that his work on the Reeves pictures was "the high water mark of my career", he decided after they were made that the headaches of big budget production were not for him. Together with comedian Harold Berens' brother, Leslie, he formed Global-Queensway Films in order to return to documentary production.

The company did make a couple of sex films including Martin Cole's notorious sex education short *Growing Up* (1971), which, to the horror of moral reformer Mary Whitehouse, showed children how to masturbate. But for the rest of the Seventies the company's sole output was short "interest" films, regularly booed off the screen in Hampstead and Kensington, but apparently accepted without murmur everywhere else. Although the demise in the mid-Eighties of the full supporting programme was regrettable, it should be remembered that at least the sponsored travelogue died with it.

While it flourished, the British sex film business was operated by a very tightly-knit community. Most of the film-makers knew each other, shared each other's actors and writers, and went to the previews of each other's films.

Lost Marks: Harrison Marks prepares Monique Devereaux and Howard Nelson for a scene in *Pattern of Evil*, never shown in Britain

But one man remained aloof from the rest of the sex trade and this was its foremost practitioner, George Harrison Marks, whose name was, and to a certain extent still is, a byword for British erotica.

Marks, who claimed recently never to have heard of his main rival, Pete Walker, stands alone in many other ways. He was the first to make a fortune out of filth. (His own claim, that he was a millionaire, is an exaggeration). He was the only pioneer from the Fifties still making sex films in the Nineties. He was one of the few directors to admit, albeit grudgingly, to having graduated to hard core pornography.* And whereas his competitors were mostly indistinguishable from the average businessman, Marks actually led the kind of life that many assume to be concomitant with "smut peddling": he was twice prosecuted for sending obscene materials through the post; he was bankrupted; and he survived four relationships (three marriages and an eight year affair with his model Pamela Green) and five years of alcoholism.

His career, however, was not devoted exclusively to sex. He produced and appeared in a slapstick comedy called *The Chimney Sweeps* (1963) and made a series of similar films for a BBC television programme for deaf children. Comedy was also the mainstay of his last films to date, *The Nine Ages of Nakedness (1969)* and *Come Play with Me* (1977), and it has been his penchant, if not his forte, since childhood.

Marks makes the unsubstantiated claim that he is distantly related to G.H. Elliott, who, until his death in 1962, was music-hall's "Chocolate Coloured Coon". Marks was still in his teens when he teamed up with a friend, Sam Stuart a.k.a. Stuart Samuels, to form Harrison and Stuart, a comedy cross-talk act which toured the halls in the late Forties.

Despite the fact that their material was pinched from other performers, the duo finally achieved a position halfway up the bills. But by that time the death knell had sounded for variety, and the strip revues were moving in. One night in Hull in 1951 Marks decided to pack it in. "When I look back on it now I think, 'Jesus Christ, what on earth did we do it for?' Well, of course we were young, we loved it, but I mean the shit we had to put up with. The digs were diabolical, the conditions backstage at some of those bloody theatres were archaic - you know, bloody gaslight in the dressing rooms. They were terrible. But, you know, you stuck it."

---

*John Lindsay, Britain's only significant hard core director, also flirted with the soft core market. He co-produced and wrote the story of *The Love Pill* (1971), a passable sex comedy about a pill that turns women into nymphomaniacs. He also co-directed *The Porn-Brokers* (1973), a survey of the European porn industry, and *The Hot Girls* (1974), a pseudo-documentary about nude modelling in Britain. His co-producer credit on another sex comedy, *I'm Not Feeling Myself Tonight!* (1975), was removed by its production company after Lindsay had been prosecuted (unsuccessfully) for producing obscene films.

Prior to his music-hall career Marks had gained some kind of film experience. According to him this was at Ealing Studios, where he learned about lighting from Czech cinematographer Otto Heller and helped the ancient cinema pioneer Cecil Hepworth, who "used to bugger about on a Moviola." Pamela Green's memory, however, is that Marks told her he lugged film cans around at Pathé News. She is reasonably sure he did not meet Otto Heller until 1959, when Marks visited the set of Green's first film *Peeping Tom*, which Heller lit. Whatever the case, Marks seems to have observed enough camera technique to enable him to switch from performing to photography.

He began by snapping his fellow comedians, one of whom, a young unknown stooging for the magician David Nixon, was Norman Wisdom. In 1952 Wisdom was chosen to appear at the Prince of Wales theatre in *Paris to Piccadilly*, the London version of the *Folies Bergère*. Marks used the Wisdom connection to gain further commissions photographing the Prince of Wales showgirls. One of these was Pamela Green.

The most famous British nude of the Fifties, Britain's answer to America's Betty Page, Green also wielded an influence over Marks, and thereby the development of British nude photography, hitherto acknowledged only by those in the trade. "Some photographers of renown," said Peter Sykes, editor of *Men Only* magazine, in 1974, "maintain that it was she who made Harrison Marks and that he would never have amounted to very much without her."

A former art student, who turned to nude modelling to pay her way through college, Green not only participated in every stage of the photographic process - from designing and painting the sets to finishing the prints - she even went so far as to dictate Marks' much-imitated style.

Doubtful about the early, unimaginative pictures he took of her, Green suggested that Marks should follow the example of Alan Duncan, a little-known but talented photographer who manipulated light and shade to sculpture and texture his models' bodies.

Together Marks and Green manufactured the most exciting British sex goddess of the Fifties. She was an illusory creature (Green adopted different personalities and worked under several pseudonyms), but her candid relationship with the camera made her chic sexuality and perfect body seem almost attainable.

The Green image was marketed firstly in sets of five photographs. Their success provided the capital for a series of magazines, beginning in 1957 with *Kamera*, which established the Marks house-style. Green was then the main attraction of the glamour films Marks began making, shortly after Stanley Long, in 1958. She was also the star of his first feature film, *Naked as Nature Intended* (1961), the most famous British nudie of them all.

Before shooting began, Marks went to the British Board of Film Censors and met Secretary John Trevelyan: "I told Trevelyan what I wanted to do. He

The crucial towels: Bridget Leonard, Pamela Green, Jackie Salt and Petrina Forsyth in *Naked As Nature Intended*

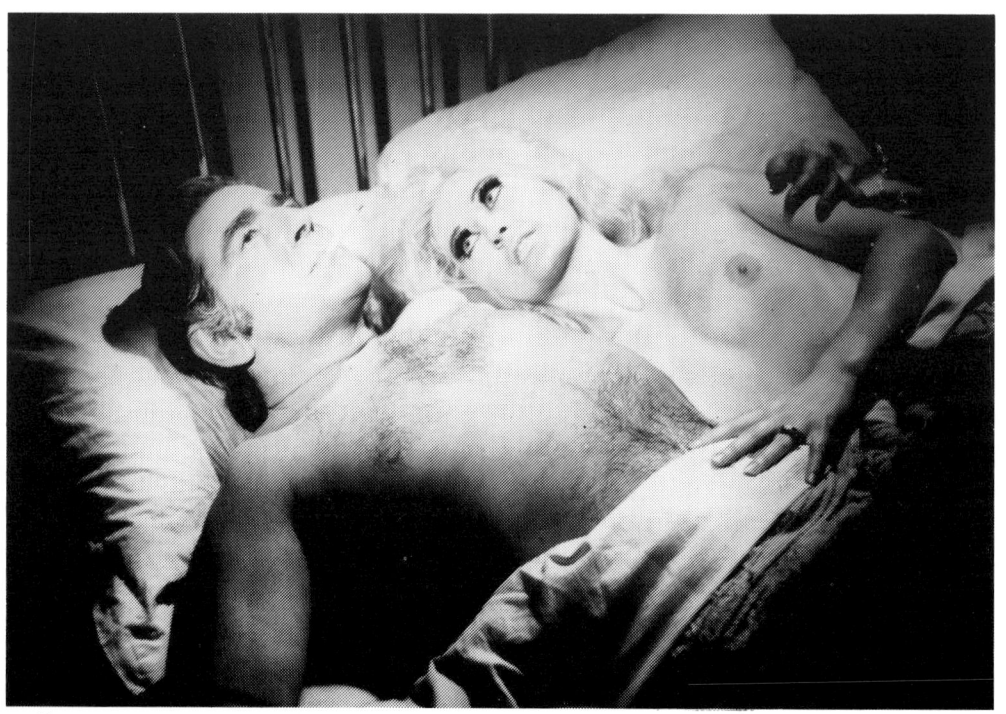

Still at it: Harrison Marks in *The Nine Ages of Nakedness*

said, 'No, no, no, no, no.' I said, 'It's going to be a genuine film about British naturism. I'm going to be waving the banner for nudists."

You were lying?

"Well, of course I was. I didn't have a script. I only had an idea. All I knew was I wanted to put nudes on the screen."

Trevelyan was finally bludgeoned into passing the film when Marks hoodwinked Charles Macaskie, the founder of the British naturist movement, to sanction its worthiness by taking part. But Trevelyan still insisted on exercising a measure of control: he cut an opening scene which included two girls discussing their forthcoming holiday while lounging in a bath towel and a baby doll nightie respectively.

"There could be a connotation that they're Lesbians," Trevelyan pronounced. Marks was astonished: "I said, 'There's nothing about Lesbianism! They're sitting looking at the map planning their holiday.' Bonk! That whole bloody scene came out."

Its removal did not affect the box-office receipts. Eighteen months after the film opened, audiences were still queueing round the block. Fifteen years after it opened, commuters could still appreciate the joke of a poster which showed a bar of Fry's Chocolate Cream without its silver foil. The caption read: *Naked As Nature Intended.*

Today the film can be appreciated as a suspense thriller almost worthy of Hitchcock. What must be an hour's worth of footage consists of a prettily photographed travelogue in which our five attractive heroines take an extremely roundabout route to Land's End for a summer holiday. Every man they meet is played by Marks' former stooge, Stuart Samuels, a featured player in many Marks movies.

Time seems to have no meaning as the girls explore a succession of tourist traps including Stonehenge and the Minnack open-air theatre in Porthcurno. At each location it seems as though clothes may be doffed, but no. Not until twenty minutes from the end does Pamela realise that there is nothing "wrong or improper or unnatural" about nudity, and off comes the inhibiting bikini. A minute longer and less robust patrons may have needed medical aid.

On the face of it, Marks appeared surprisingly reluctant to move with the times and introduce more explicit sex into his films. In 1965 he made *The Naked World of Harrison Marks* and in 1969, a full six years after rival companies had stopped producing nudies, Marks' *The Nine Ages of Nakedness* appeared. How could Marks, of all people, develop such an apparent coyness?

"Because sex bores the arse off me. That's basically it. It's not my bag. My mind runs to comedy. And my track record shows that a mixture of comedy and pretty birds wins."

Harrison Marks finds sex boring?

Come Play with Me: the starlets playing with Harrison Marks and Alfie Bass include Mary Millington (far left) and Suzy Mandel (centre back)

One of the most successful British films of 1976

London in the Raw startles Birmingham

London in the Raw: Playboy Bunny Girls, prepared for exposure by Stanley Long, are captured in this photo by John Lindsay, later to become Britain's leading pornographer

"Hang on, I don't mean in that respect. I like fucking as much as anyone else. Not as much as I used to, but I still like it. But unless you make a wonderfully clever sex film with real integrity - short of that they're crap and utterly boring, and I don't think I'm ever going to make the great masterpiece so I'd rather stick to what I know."

Marks' preference for the depiction of sex as little more than an asexual prank was, as he rightly claims, what made his films so popular. That his empire collapsed in 1971 was due not to his old-fashioned British reserve, but more to his failure to handle the success it brought him.

By the turn of the Sixties his combined operations - which included a film company with its own studio in London's Holborn area, and a publishing house turning out books, magazines and calendars - had brought him prosperity, but only fleetingly. He spent as fast as he earned while the business administration went to the dogs. "When we were riding high, George suddenly seemed to lose all interest in the business, and the efficiency declined," said Green, who walked out in 1961. His second pornography trial (at the Old Bailey in 1971) was followed by five virtually fallow years during which time Marks drank himself almost literally to death.

It was David Sullivan who was responsible for Marks' return to feature films. Marks had been selling transparencies to Sullivan's sex magazines *Playbirds* and *Whitehouse*, and one evening the publisher asked Marks why he hadn't made any movies lately. Marks replied that as a matter of fact he had a script ready to go into production, but lacked the £83,000 to achieve this.

Sullivan studied Marks' budget. "How soon do we start?" the publisher enquired. "As soon as I get £20,000 pre-production money upfront," Marks replied. A few hours later he received a cheque.

This was how *Come Play with Me* (1977) came into being. An antediluvian story about comic forgers, it featured a song and dance routine by Alfie Bass and Marks himself, brief turns from such wizened troupers as Rita Webb and Cardew (The Cad) Robinson, and even briefer appearances by Sullivan's protégée Mary Millington, then called the British Linda Lovelace.

Tantalisingly previewed in Sullivan's publications, the film caused even more of a stir when, during production, a story was leaked that some of the pensioners in the cast were displeased by the film's pornographic sequences. Marks now denounces this as pure fiction:

"Bollocks. It was all bollocks. It was all instigated by Sullivan. There were a couple of sequences stronger than the ones shown in this country, but not much stronger. Of course from the word go Sullivan put out this story that we're making the most pornographic film since *Deep Throat*. It got publicity, but it nearly bloody drove me mad because I had the unions on my back and bloody Scotland Yard coming down.

"Some Equity [the actors' union] idiot came down on the set when we were involved in quite a difficult scene, and I'd just about had enough. I said, 'Yes, as a matter of fact we are making a porn film. Alfie Bass fucks the arse off Irene Handl in the next scene. Do you want to stay and watch it?' He looked at me and pissed off."

Grossing half a million pounds from its four year London run alone, *Come Play with Me* was the last blockbuster of Britain's sex film era. David Sullivan went on producing films until he was virtually the only one doing so. But Harrison Marks was not offered another opportunity to direct for the cinema in this country.

When the invitation came to direct hard core on the Continent, he at first declined and finally submitted when Germany's leading porn producer presented him with a suitcase full of Deutschmarks. The films that resulted from this deal must still remain a mystery. "I don't know whether I want to talk about them," said Marks. "I made films for Germany and Denmark. Let's leave it at that. O.K.?"

Marks still works out of the North London flat where he was born in 1926. He still produces magazines and videos of a type that helped make his name nearly 35 years ago. That name still ensures brisk sales "mainly in America". But instead of Pamela Green showing her undies, the sex queens are now Spanking Schoolgirls and Nurses in Rubber.

Don't tell Mr Grimsdale: Norman Wisdom and Sally Geeson in *What's Good for the Goose*

Chapter 3: "The Grafters"

The "nudie" era which activated the British sex film industry may have had built-in obsolescence, but it lasted a good deal longer than cynics predicted. *Nudist Paradise* appeared in 1958; the last nudie, *The Reluctant Nudist*, was made in 1963, and old nudist pictures were still being re-released until the end of the Sixties.

They often played as supports to art-house features. *Take Off Your Clothes and Live* was coupled with Jean-Luc Godard's *Une femme mariée*. It seems that, for patrons of the period, a turn-on was a turn-on whether it was bouncing breasts on the volleyball court or *nouvelle vague* close-ups of thumb joints.

Throughout their life-span the nudist films' formula - asexual sun worship - remained virtually unaltered. There were one or two exceptions. Walter Slaney's *Nude and Variations* (1958) boasted the censor-appeasing presence of the sculptress Elizabeth Frink and therefore was able to feature what one startled critic described as "surprisingly suggestive poses." And in a somewhat desperate attempt to ring the changes Michael Keatering's *Eves on Skis* (1963) substituted snow for sand and dragooned goose-pimpled naturists into building an igloo.

Generally, however, British film-makers were forced to remain within the bounds of decency defined by the B.B.F.C. The Board flatly refused to allow the exhibition of the nude comedies and melodramas which, in the United States, had superseded the naturist documentary as a result of the success of Russ Meyer's epoch-making sex film *The Immoral Mr Teas* (1959).

The first film of this type to creep into Britain was *Career Girl* (1959) starring June Wilkinson, a heavily cut version of which was passed by some authorities in 1963. The work of Russ Meyer was not seen here until the highly unrepresentative *Fanny Hill* was screened in 1966. Incredibly, *Mr Teas* has never had a British release.

British films dealing with any aspect of sexuality other than the evils of prostitution were extreme rarities until 1963. Prior to that time *Too Young to Love* and *Never Take Sweets from a Stranger* (both 1959) had dealt discreetly with under-age sex and child molestation respectively; impotency had been handled with somewhat less integrity by Sidney J. Furie in *During One Night* (1961); and, as previously noted, *Mary Had a Little* (1961) had been Britain's first faltering attempt at a sex comedy.

But independent sexploitation in a recognisable form did not appear until Robert Hartford-Davis made *The Yellow Teddybears* in 1963. Active in movies since 1939, Hartford-Davis made cheap exploitation films of all kinds - sex dramas, horror movies and even an unreleased pop musical *Gonks Go Beat* - until he went to Hollywood and became one of only two British sex film makers (the other is Martin Campbell) to graduate to mainstream cinema.

Many of his early British films were written by Derek Ford, who developed into one of the country's most prolific grafters when the sex film business reached its zenith in the Seventies. Unlike his contemporaries, fast buck merchants most of whom slid into soft porn from the related fields of theatre and still photography, Ford is a quietly-spoken man of letters with extensive training in radio, television and "straight" cinema.

Born near Tilbury in Essex in 1932, he wrote his first play, in collaboration with his elder brother Donald, for BBC radio's *Children's Hour* in 1948. The brothers continued writing for radio while Derek ran errands for the public relations firm that introduced espresso coffee to London. He was then called up for his National Service (he chose the Army and was posted to Germany), and, after his demob, joined a tinpot film outfit run by Morton Lewis.

Between 1955 and 1960, while the company moved into the experimental field of TV commercials, Derek Ford worked his way up from clapper boy to a partner in the firm. It was he who thought up the name "Iced Diamond" to describe a new line of Hotpoint refrigerators. But Lewis would not let Ford direct, and this was one of the disagreements which led eventually to Ford walking out in a huff.

He became a director immediately.* Within days of quitting his job, he was on his way to Paris, having been given £500 to salvage an unedited Swedish sex film called *Svenska flickor i Paris*. After looking at the material, Ford re-wrote the script, shot some extra footage and, in removing one of the sub-plots, cut out the part played by a little-known actor named Jean-Paul Belmondo.

In 1961 the film had a successful run in London as *Paris Playgirls*. Recalling his handiwork, Ford says, "Apparently it was a very depressing film in Swedish. But it was quite a funny film when it opened here."

Ford was then invited to go to Ibiza to direct *Los tres que robbaran una banco* (1961), a Swedish-Spanish co-production about three old peasants who become bank robbers. Arbitrating daily in the scorching sun between the Swedish crew and the Spanish cast left Ford so disenchanted with the glamour of moviemaking that, as soon as the film was completed, he fled back to England to resume his writing partnership with his brother, this time under the auspices of Michael Klinger and Tony Tenser.

The godfathers of British sexploitation, Klinger and Tenser were connected in some way with virtually every sex film maker in the business. *En*

---

* Morton Lewis also went on to direct a sex film, the atrocious *Secrets of a Superstud* (1976).

Sexploitation arrives. *The Yellow Teddybears*...

... and *Saturday Night Out*

passant they also produced films directed by Roman Polanski, Michael Reeves, David Bailey and many other young talents.

Klinger managed London's famous Nell Gwynn strip club, and Tenser was the head of publicity for Miracle Films (he was the first to label Brigitte Bardot the "sex kitten".) In 1960 the pair went into business together to open the Compton Cinema Club, which screened uncertificated "new wave" films like *Private Property* and *Dentonville* before switching to "soft core porn" (although this term was not in common use until 1971.)

Compton-Cameo Films later distributed and produced movies before the company was disbanded in 1969. Klinger quickly went "respectable", producing big-budget action adventures like *Gold* and *Shout at the Devil*, but Tenser remained a sleaze-merchant. He set up Tigon Films, which produced and distributed dozens of low-grade exploitation films, notably *What's Good for the Goose* (1969), the sex comedy that finished Norman Wisdom's film career. In the Seventies Tenser left the business to run a company manufacturing cane furniture.

Tenser could sniff out a commercial proposition with more ease than most. In 1963 he read a newspaper report about a group of schoolgirls who had taken to advertising the loss of their virginity by wearing the golliwog brooches given away as a sales gimmick by the Robertson jam company.

This story was given to the Fords to flesh out into a movie. The finished product was not quite what the devious Tenser had in mind. Being, at that time, writers of integrity, the Fords came up with a social drama which questioned the methods of sex education in schools. But Tenser needn't have worried. The edifying treatment of a scandalous theme impressed the censors, and attracted not only sensation-seekers, but also head teachers who took their sixth-formers in the hope that the film would be an Awful Warning. Finally titled *The Yellow Teddybears* (Robertsons, not unexpectedly, had refused to allow their trademark to be besmirched), it did big business.

Nevertheless, the Fords were subsequently required to write less sociological material. *Saturday Night Out* (1963) was about the sexual adventures of six merchant seamen. It featured the Liverpool pop group The Searchers, who happened to be in London at the time. Compton-Cameo could have had The Beatles, but didn't want to pay their fare from Liverpool.

The Black Torment (1964) and *Corruption* (1965) were two notably sophisticated horror films (*Corruption*, a blood-curdling re-working of Franju's *Eyes without a Face*, is long overdue for rediscovery as a masterpiece of British Grand Guignol.)

In 1971, having penned seven feature films, three television plays, and nearly fifty episodes of such TV series as *Z Cars*, *The Saint* and *Adam Adamant*, Donald and Derek Ford decided to stop writing together. Donald, formerly Chairman of the London County Council's General Purposes Com-

The Wife Swappers: it made more than *Spartacus*

mittee, had been appointed a magistrate at London's Bow Street Court, a post he held for more than ten years. It's amusing to think that petty criminals were probably unaware they were being sentenced by the man who wrote *The Yellow Teddybears*. Donald Ford died in 1991.

For Derek Ford the front door to the movie industry may have closed, but the back door opened: he renewed his acquaintance with Stanley Long, and within hours the two men had set up a sex film which Ford would direct.

Although Ford maintains that "I've never made the films I wanted to make. I've always ended up getting sidetracked," he seems to have had all the prerequisites to make it big in British sex films. Having overcome his inclination to make meaningful statements, he was now of the opinion that for him writing was a trade, not an art, and was surrendering to his desire to "turn everything into farce."

His training in television had forced him to churn out simple scripts to be shot on low budgets. And since directors like Hartford-Davis had followed his scenarios to the letter, even acting on his suggestions for camera angles, Ford knew that he had accumulated enough technical experience to return to the director's chair himself.

Of the three films Ford and Long made together, the most significant was the third, *The Wife Swappers* (1969), one of the biggest-grossing British sex films of all time. During its opening week in one London cinema, it took £4,200 at the box-office. The inflation-adjusted equivalent today would be £31,000. Compare this to the mere £23,039 which the 1991 re-issue of *Spartacus* took during its first week at the Odeon, Marble Arch. Or the £39,701 which Mel Brooks' *Life Stinks* scraped together in three days from 59 screens throughout Britain.*

The appeal of *The Wife Swappers*, a "dramatised documentary", which Ford based on the experiences of his swinging friends, lay in its timely exploitation of group sex, a (largely provincial) social trend, the idea of which, for obvious reasons, was equally titillating for men and women. Consequently *The Wife Swappers* became one of the only British sex films to attract large audiences of couples.

It is hard to find a trashier example of the genre than *The Wife Swappers*. (Hard, but not impossible: Kenneth Rowles' *Take an Easy Ride* [1976] is worse.) When *The Wife Swappers* was first shown to the press, they were aghast. "It stinks," said *The People*. "The British film industry should be ashamed of itself," declared the *Daily Sketch*. "So badly written and so terribly acted... it could become one of the funniest films of the year," was the *Daily Mirror*'s prediction.

* Perhaps the most invidious comparison to be made is with *Blonde Fist*, one of the very rare examples of low-budget British film production to be released in 1991. Its cumulative gross, before being hastily withdrawn from four London screens, was £2,502.

Correctly assuming the film to be a low-cost production, *New Society* ournalist Clive Jordan guessed the budget to be "around the £50,000 mark," an estimate which greatly flattered Ford and Long since they'd brought the film in for £16,000.

Even its makers cannot bear to be reminded of *The Wife Swappers*. "It would give me the horrors to see that one again," admitted Ford. Long agreed. "I think it's dreadful," he said, but emphasised that this wasn't purely because of the "abysmal" acting*: "It was moralising, which made it banal," he explained.

"But it had to be that way because even in 1969 we were still having to add disapproving commentaries saying, 'Look at this, please, but it's terrible, isn't it?' This was just to get the films through the censor because it was all right providing you didn't approve of what you were showing.

"We had these dreadful bloody advisory psychiatrists explaining the social behaviour patterns and all that crap, which no one was interested in in the slightest. I remember taking a psychiatrist up to see John Trevelyan and trying to convince him that the purpose of making *The Wife Swappers* was not to make money, but to try and improve society. It was a charade."

When Derek Ford left Stanley Long to work with another producer, Tony Tenser's former associate Michael Green, his first instinct was to wring a little more mileage out of the evidently enticing theme of sin in the suburbs. *Suburban Wives* (1971) and *Commuter Husbands* (1972) did well enough despite having to do battle with a glut of German films (particularly the interminable *Hausfrauen-Report* series) on the same subject.

Ford also made *Secret Rites* (1971), a documentary about the bizarre activities of Alex Sanders, self-styled King of the Witches, and *Sex Express* (1975) starring Heather Deeley, a nymphette whose personal problems prevented her from fulfilling her early promise as Britain's sex queen of the Seventies.

But Ford's best-known films of the Seventies were sex comedies. *Keep It Up, Jack!* (1973) was an archetypal British sex romp involving music-hall, drag, rude puns (the title is an example) and virtually no sex. The stars were Mark Jones and Sue Longhurst, who had hardly any ability, either as comedians or as romantic leads, and consequently appeared in more British sex films than any other actors. Longhurst, a former schoolteacher, and Jones, who once worked with the Royal Shakespeare Company (he was the Abbot in *The Marat/Sade*) were still making sex films as late as 1979, when they appeared together in Ray Selfe's *Can I Come Too?*

Ford's last sex films were the comedies *What's Up Nurse* (1977) and its sequel *What's Up Superdoc* (1978). Their bedpan humour was as infallible as

---

* One of the stars was Larry Taylor, later to become "Captain Birdseye".

always with the public, and no doubt the series would have continued had it not been for escalating costs. In seven years Ford's budgets had risen from £16,000 to £80,000. The sex film was no longer economically viable.

Ford attempted to get back into the big time. He had seen Eddie Kidd interviewed on TV, been impressed with his personality, and written a movie script for the stunt rider called *Bikers*. The ubiquitous Michael Klinger took an interest in the project, but felt he wouldn't be able to raise any cash for it on the strength of Ford's tarnished reputation. Ford was eased out, TV commercial director Ross Cramer was brought in, and *Bikers*, a £500,000 programmer, mushroomed into *Riding High* (1980), a £3 million catastrophe.

"Are we really going to discuss that?" Ford asked me. "What was heartbreaking," he finally admitted, "was that Eddie Kidd risked his life. That last scene, where he jumped over the broken bridge, that was an eighty foot jump. Nobody had ever done that before and he didn't know if he was going to make it and we certainly didn't. That's why it was the last shot in the picture, and I had two alternative endings - one where he lived and one where he died. And to think he did that - he risked his life for such a lousy picture. That's what broke my heart, I mean I felt so guilty about that. When he called me [in 1982] and said, 'I'm getting married. Will you come to the wedding?', I thought, 'Thank Christ, he's forgiven me.'"

Derek Ford was one of three directors whose work dominated the exploitation market during the Seventies. Ford and Stanley Long manufactured safe, conventional, technically adequate product that consequently attracted no interest outside the raincoat trade. But the third man, Pete Walker, chose such unusual themes and developed them with such stylishly resourceful use of his modest budgets that he eventually drew favourable notices in the *Financial Times*, attracted a small cult following, and was referred to as Britain's Russ Meyer. He was without doubt this country's most talented director of exploitation films, but he blew his only opportunity of progressing to something better.

In an effort to drag his achievements before a wider audience during the past twenty years, I have written more about Pete Walker than any other director, although I freely admit that not all of this has been true.

When I first met him in 1972, he spent several hours narrating a version of his life story which I dutifully reported and only later discovered to be somewhat fanciful. But he is so genuinely sensitive about his image that to start disputing some of his claims would be churlish, and so for now, at least, the biography which appeared in the December, 1974, issue of *Films & Filming* must stand. This précis is probably accurate.

The son of Syd Walker, the popular comic monologuist of radio's *Band Waggon* (1938-39), Peter left his home town of Brighton in the early Fifties and arrived in London hoping to follow in his father's footsteps. His first major

Pete Walker: he could have been a contender

"That was a great title. You could just see them reaching for their raincoats" (Pete Walker)

appearance as a stand-up comic was probably at Collins' music-hall in Islington, North London, and for as long as I've known him, Walker has insisted that "It was Wednesday night, second house, before I got my first laugh."

Despite this lack of aptitude, Walker toured in music-hall for some time, later moving on to repertory, for which he seems to have been equally unsuited ("I was terrible, a dreadful actor.") He also played bit parts in films although his only appearances to have been confirmed are as a casino manager in *The Breaking Point* (1959) and as a party guest in Michael Winner's short *Behave Yourself* (1962).*

At some time in the early Sixties he went to the U.S.A. for the first time, but what he did there remains unclear. When he returned to Britain, however, he

---

* Walker later played unbilled cameos in his own films and appeared briefly, driving his own Rolls Royce, in his friend Stanley Long's *Adventures of a Taxi Driver* (1975).

became heavily involved in the production of glamour films, making over four hundred home movies ("all terrible, all shot within half-an-hour") in the Heritage range.

Although a late arrival on the glamour film scene (Stanley Long and Harrison Marks had preceded him by four years), Walker did well enough out of it to finance his first feature, *I Like Birds*, shot in six days in 1966 for £6,740. A seedy comedy about the head of an East Grinstead puritan group, who leads a double life as a sex magazine editor, it was released in 1967 as a second feature to *Pretty Polly* starring Hayley Mills.

Walker's next three films gave little indication of a skinflick *auteur* in the making. *Strip Poker* (1968), written between seven o'clock one night and two o'clock the following morning, is a crude gangster melodrama with bursts of unappetising nudity. *School For Sex* (1968) is a puerile comedy about a divorcee who teaches girls to swindle rich men in return for ten per cent of their takings. It led me to write: "It's hard to see how anybody in his right mind could let Pete Walker anywhere near a camera." Nevertheless it became one of Walker's biggest international successes.

Man of Violence (1969), the last film Walker used to learn his craft, was in his own words, "a glossy Hollywood thriller made for three and a half pence with the necessary ingredients - Luan Peters with her 42 inch bust, and a bit of blood." ("I *haven't* got a 42 inch bust!" Miss Peters complained when she first read this.)

In 1971, when I was the Assistant Editor of the British Film Institute's *Monthly Film Bulletin*, I remember the annoyance I felt when one of our writers, Paul Joannides, flew in the face of current critical opinion by describing Pete Walker's latest film *Cool It Carol!* as "beguilingly good-humoured." But when I saw the picture myself I found to my astonishment that he was right; and, in retrospect, I think that *Carol* is probably the best British sex film ever made.

It came about when Walker was approached by the writer Murray Smith, who gave him a one and a half page synopsis based on a story he'd read in the previous Sunday's *News of the World*. It concerned two teenagers who had gone astray after being attracted to the lights of the big city; the girl had become a prostitute and the boy was arrested for living off her immoral earnings.

Sensibly scripted by Smith, efficiently photographed by Peter Jessop (who went on to become sexploitation's most sought-after cameraman) and generally well-performed (although Robin Askwith over-acts), *Cool It Carol!* is a self-aware sex comedy, slick and witty. And it can now be seen as a true reflection of the change in moral standards that had arrived with the turn of the Seventies, one which was vigorously resisted by critics of the period, who dismissed *Carol* as "nauseous", "repulsive" and "a thoroughly nasty bit of pornography."

Barry Evans: her husband came home unexpectedly

Luan Peters hasn't got a 42 inch bust

Die Screaming, Marianne, also released in 1971, confirmed Walker's potential as a low-budget stylist, and after I saw this Hitchcockian thriller shot largely on location in the Algarve, I asked if he would grant me an interview. He was already quite rich and had a Rolls with electrically-operated windows, which I had never seen before.

He gave me some wonderful quotes, all perfectly in keeping with the British sex film producer mentality ("I've always believed in antiseptic sex", "I hate tits. Horrible things", "95% of the world's population have *Coronation Street* mentalities. They don't notice that girls don't deliver lines properly. All right, I notice, it worries me, it grates on me. But I don't think it worries these funny people in Wigan and Scunthorpe.")

At the time Walker was completing *The Four Dimensions of Greta* (1972), the first British sex film in 3-D. I have a feeling he wanted to advertise it with the line "A boob in your lap!" I reported that it featured "the most frenzied display of mass nudity and sexual gymnastics yet seen on British screens", but I can no longer remember any of this, only that the attempts to project Lena Skoog's breasts over the heads of the audience were not entirely successful.

After further experimentation, the stereoscopic effects improved in Walker's next film, *The Flesh and Blood Show* (1972), an old-fashioned whodunnit set in an Old Dark Theatre. But although it was the peep-show gimmickry that drew the crowds to these two films (huge crowds in the case of *Greta*), it was Walker's increasingly tongue-in-cheek intensity that set them apart from run-of-the-mill sexploitation.

In both cases the plots are ludicrous, but knowingly camped-up. At the height of the mayhem in *Greta*, Walker had the hero exclaim, "This is just like a very cheap British sex film!" Such fun at the expense of the earnest British punter was not common in 1972.

In *Tiffany Jones* (1973), an adaptation of the newspaper comic strip, Walker tried for a more sophisticated sex comedy, but the script was leaden and the film, a failure, was eventually released as a second-feature. Looking for a new approach, Walker settled on Gothic horror and filched the construction of *Psycho* for a kinky thriller, *House of Whipcord* (1974), in which two ageing lunatics capture young girls and take them to their private prison on the moors to be starved, whipped and hanged.

"It deserves to become a horror classic due to its claustrophobic and unnerving atmosphere," I said when interviewed in 1981, and although the film has yet to achieve such veneration, it did succeed in attracting serious critical attention, albeit from those reviewers with a taste for sado-masochism.

Walker had always insisted that, as soon as his pictures started getting good notices, he'd stop making them. But when it came to the crunch, he went back on his word. He was secretly pleased by the favourable response to *Whipcord* and began planning films in a similar vein, "terror movies" without sex, which

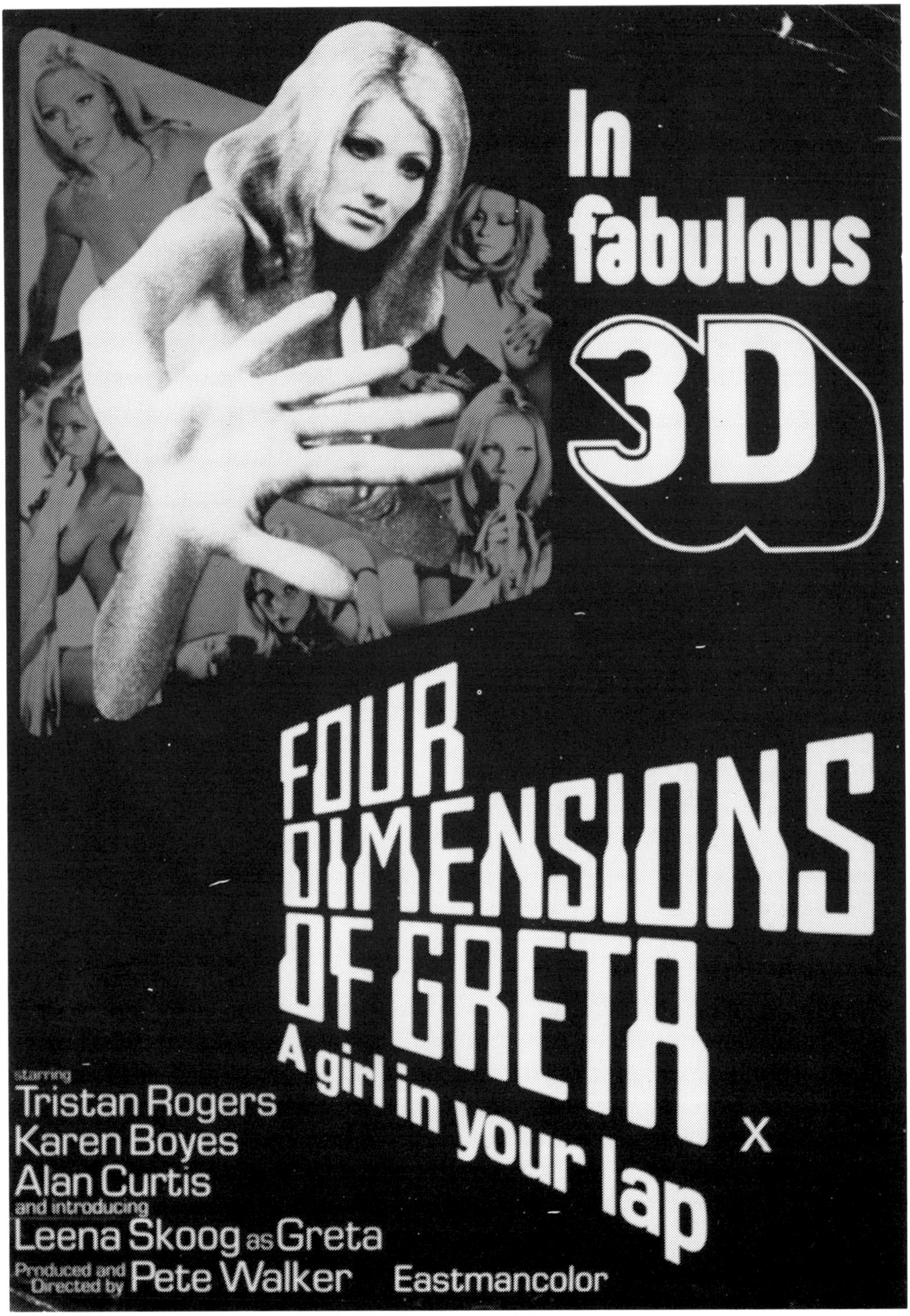
In fabulous 3D
FOUR DIMENSIONS OF GRETA
A girl in your lap
X
starring
Tristan Rogers
Karen Boyes
Alan Curtis
and introducing
Leena Skoog as Greta
Produced and Directed by Pete Walker
Eastmancolor

would provide his ticket out of the exploitation league.

These films consolidated his "cult" reputation. They were screened at the National Film Theatre, and Walker got his name in Halliwell's *Filmgoer's Companion*. But this kudos was won at the expense of box-office success. Released some years before the stalk-and-slash vogue initiated by *Halloween*, the terror films were not widely popular, and the last, *The Comeback* (1977) made such losses that Walker was left with no option but to return to sexploitation.

Home Before Midnight (1978), about schoolgirl sex, turned the clock back in a way that surprised many of Walker's followers. Thematically it was almost as if he had gone full circle to the days of *School for Sex*, while the pervasive presence of a Moral Standpoint (society's fear of sex for the under-sixteens is irrational) recalled *The Yellow Teddybears* and the dawn of the British sex film. Ten years earlier it would have been a scorcher, but in 1978 it was a problem picture. Premiered after a year's delay, it was later put on a double-bill with an old *Sweeney* film.

Embittered that he listened to his footsteps walking out of the industry, Walker apparently finds it painful to discuss the old days, and is suspicious of anyone who brings up the subject. When I asked him in 1982 about the female image he was trying to put across in his glamour films, he exploded, "Why are you going into all this? I know exactly the kind of article you're trying to get out of this and I really don't think I want to be involved in it honestly. I mean the whole thing's a put-down, isn't it?"

I was not allowed to continue speaking to him until I switched off my tape recorder. Later he refused to supply stills to illustrate my article. I heard that when he read it he was not pleased. I have neither seen nor spoken to him ever since.

What Walker kept from me throughout our last meeting was that he was planning what was to be his final film. If the fates had been kinder, *House of the Long Shadows* (1982) could easily have made Pete Walker the most famous director in this book. It was, by the standards of the day, a high-concept horror film uniting for the first time in screen history four legends of the genre, Vincent Price, Peter Cushing, Christopher Lee and John Carradine. They should have been joined by a fifth, Elsa Lanchester, but she was too ill to make the trip to England.

As it turned out, however, the film did nothing for anybody's reputation. Based on a hoary old stage melodrama, the story took ages to get going and never supplied the shocks and suspense the post-*Halloween* crowd had come to expect.

Interviewed in 1991 I opined that Walker was "a man of his time" but that *House of the Long Shadows* "proved that time had marched on." I still stand by this.

Christopher Neil and Prudence Drage in *Adventures of a Plumber's Mate*. He's now a record producer; she works for a solicitor

Gavin Campbell (centre) in *The Playbirds* before he became a presenter on the BBC television consumer programme *That's Life!*

Chapter 4: "The Final Days"

"Sex bores the arse off me" (Harrison Marks, 1982)

"I hate tits. Horrible things" (Pete Walker, 1972)

"Sexploitation films are just too boring for words" (Derek Ford, 1970)

"Pornography doesn't turn me on" (Stanley Long, 1982)

Encapsulated in these quotes from Britain's foremost sexploitation directors is the cause of the British sex film's woeful lack of eroticism. Though certainly true of some, it would be an inaccurate generalisation to suggest that Britain's sex film makers did not enjoy sex *per se*, but it is a fact that in most cases they were either offended by the industry in which they found themselves or, at the very least, performed their tasks without enthusiasm. Stanley Long elaborates:

"A sex scene really takes quite a long time to do properly, but we tended to regard it as an ancilliary thing you bashed off in the last ten minutes of shooting when everybody looked tired and bored."

Some directors made no secret of the distaste they felt for the genre. I have seen Joe McGrath, the comedy director who was occasionally forced into earning a crust from sexploitation, direct a sex scene with his back to the set; he turned round once to mutter an instruction I have never forgotten: "Move your bum up and down a bit, Curtis."

McGrath and many other directors have disowned their sex films by assuming pseudonyms on the credits. McGrath was once "Croisette Meubles", Derek Robbins' alias was "Sam Spade", and Gerry O'Hara has masqueraded as both "Billy White" and "Lawrence Britton".

Other film-makers seemed reluctant to admit their involvement in soft porn even to themselves. Donovan Winter once told me in great earnest that he considered his production *The Deadly Females* to be *film noir*, and when I included Lindsay Shonteff, the director of *Permissive* and *The Yes Girls*, in a piece on the sex film business written for the trade paper *Screen International*, Shonteff rang the editor threatening to sue.

Antipathy within the business was deep-rooted. By the mid-Sixties the B.B.F.C. had allowed sex and nudity to be combined in a few "quality" pictures*, and was being forced to grant equal rights to exploitation films. But

---

* Sexual frankness in British films is generally traced back to *Room at the Top* (1958), but there was no nudity in a major British film until *A Kind of Loving* (1961).

recruits for the emergent sex film industry were hard to find, and until the end of the Seventies the nudie and glamour film pioneers had the field largely to themselves.

One of the first of the new boys was Norman J. Warren, an editor who, in 1965, had made an art house short called *Fragment*. It was to be his one and only sortie upmarket. *Fragment* was seen by Calcutta-born Bachoo Sen, a distributor/producer who felt Warren was the man to direct a sex film he was planning. Made in 1967 as *Her Private Hell*, it was the product of an almost comical prudishness: Warren hated directing the bedroom scenes and was in the good company of a leading lady who didn't want to take off her clothes in case her mother found out.

Yet such was his enthusiasm for film-making that Warren agreed to direct a follow-up, *Loving Feeling* (1968), which introduced a new French sex kitten, Françoise Pascal, to British screens, and also included a hastily-written scene on a beach which must rank among the most embarrassing ever shown in public. It would be wonderful to see it again.

Unable to face the prospect of a third sex film, Warren did not work again until 1976, when *Satan's Slave* led to a string of low-budget horror movies in which sex was often a prominent feature. After Warren's departure Bachoo Sen produced *Love Is a Splendid Illusion* (1969), directed by Tom Clegg, who, much later, progressed to cops-and-robbers adventures like *Sweeney 2* and *McVicar*. Sen went on to become a junior league sex movie mogul, producing films, distributing them and exhibiting them at two London cinemas he owned. "Is it true," I asked Warren, "that, when you were working for Bachoo Sen, you were paid £30 a week?" "Not as much as that," he replied.

As sex film production increased towards the end of the Sixties, there appeared on the scene a handful of directors with what could be described as a modicum of talent. In 1969 the actor John Bown wrote and directed *Monique*, a polished sex drama with surprisingly accomplished performances, although the quality of the sex scenes, butchered by the censor, was difficult to judge.

Malcolm Leigh drew a number of good notices for his sex comedy *Games That Lovers Play* (1970), starring a young Joanna Lumley. Shortly after the film's release, when it was announced that Leigh would direct Björn Andresen (the boy from *Death in Venice*) and Lynn Redgrave in a big budget drama *How Lovely Are the Messengers*, it seemed that the fabled journey from porn to art was to be made quite without effort. But as it happened Leigh fell at the first hurdle: his project collapsed days before shooting was due to begin in 1971, and he has been mysteriously untraceable ever since.

The industry's most colourful character at this time was Antony Balch. By calling he was an experimental film-maker, but by trade he was a distributor, a job he acquired under unusual circumstances. At the Cinémathèque in Paris

Joanna Lumley, before she became a New Avenger

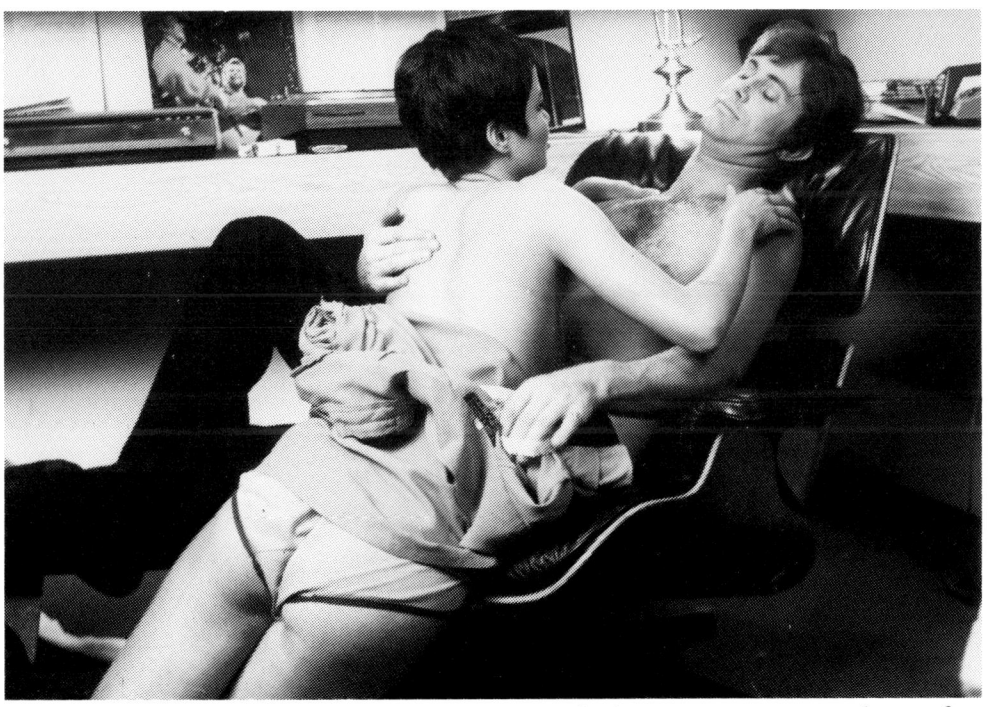

The label says Carnaby Cavern: Simon Brent helps Françoise Pascal out of her mini-skirt in *Loving Feeling*

Secrets of Sex: Mike Britton and Cathy Howard about to be censored

Loving Feeling: Simon Brent and Paula Patterson in the memorable beach scene

he saw Tod Browning's *Freaks* (1932), which had been banned in Britain for more than 30 years. "Raymond Rohauer, who held the rights at that time, asked me if I was a distributor," said Balch. "I said no, but I'll become one to show *Freaks*."

Balch's particular talent as a distributor lay in enhancing obscure foreign sex films by the appendage of meaningless yet enticing English titles - *Käpy selän alla* was released as *Skin Skin*; *Per una valigia piene di donne* became *The Kinky Darlings*; and so on. But because of his more offbeat attractions (apart from *Freaks* he also arranged the first British screenings of Samuel Fuller's *Shock Corridor*), he ingratiated himself with the critical élite. Consequently his first feature as a director, *Secrets of Sex* (1969), became the only British sex film to be reviewed in the egghead film journal *Sight and Sound* ("Above average sexploitation film, wittily scripted and agreeably irreverent.")

Much of *Secrets of Sex* was in fact stupid and badly acted, but, like Balch himself, it was perverse and outrageous and confounded censors and public alike. There has been no other British film like it, before or since. To everyone's great sorrow, Balch died in 1980 without fulfilling his ambition to film William Burroughs' *The Naked Lunch*. This was to be David Cronenberg's achievement in 1991.

"Sex education" films, of which there was a spate at the turn of the Seventies, were, of course, nothing of the sort. They were merely a ploy, like the nudist pictures of a decade earlier, to induce the British censors to pass material which would have been rejected from the average general release; and, like their nudie predecessors, the sex education producers strengthened their cause by claiming to be crusaders for truth and enlightenment.

Sex education in British cinema began in 1956, when the B.B.F.C. awarded an "X" certificate to a heavily cut version of *Birth without Fear*. (Earlier in the year the Board had banned the 1938 production *Birth of a Baby*.)

Few attempts were made to exploit this subject again until 1968, when a German film, *Helga*, went to such lengths to proclaim its unimpeachable motives that it was passed in the "A" category. There followed the inevitable avalanche of increasingly explicit sex education movies, one of which, Sweden's *More About the Language of Love*, was raided by the police in 1974. The genre then fizzled out, but made a surprising comeback in 1991 when the video-cassette *The Lovers' Guide* appeared in chain stores as a novelty item for the Christmas market.

The first British producer to wriggle through the sex education loophole was the photographer David Grant, who, in 1969 (and under the pseudonym Terry Gould) directed a film of his best-selling picture-book *Love Variations*. Almost disconcerting in its clinicality, the film possessed one sensational point of appeal - full frontal nudity, a condition which had been glimpsed on only two previous occasions in British films. The subjects then were Gillian Hills and Jane Birkin, whose pubic hair was fleetingly visible (and reputedly much snipped by randy projectionists) in *Blow Up* (1967), and Oliver Reed and Alan Bates, who stripped off in the dim firelight of Ken Russell's *Women in Love* (1969).

On the strength of Carol Jones' (and, to a lesser extent, Derek Tracey's) genitals, *Love Variations* coasted to success and provided the foundations for a sex movie empire which Grant controlled throughout the Seventies. From palatial offices, now occupied by the Trocadero in London's Piccadilly, Grant ran a group of companies which owned sex cinemas, distributed foreign sex films, and produced rudimentary sex comedies often starring John Hamill, a beefcake actor from the TV soap opera *Crossroads*.

Never a financial wizard, Grant lost thousands investing in disastrous "straight" films, particularly the notorious *The Great McGonagall* (1974) starring Peter Sellers and Spike Milligan. He withdrew from the cinema business at the end of the Seventies and moved into video with even more appalling consequences. In 1984 he was jailed for eighteen months for distributing a "video nasty". He then escaped abroad. If he is still alive, he is unlikely to return to the U.K., where he still faces sixteen charges of fraud and two of conspiracy in relation to video piracy.

The end of the Sixties saw the end of the British sex film as the exclusive province of the back-street money-grubber. As the new decade turned, the pickings had become too rich for the establishment to ignore and they leaped in to sex movie production with alacrity.

Hammer films, which had previously used symbolism to convey the eroticism of the vampire myth, suddenly became sexually explicit. Carmilla is a Lesbian vampire who kisses as she kills in the effectively spooky *The Vampire Lovers* (1970), based on a Sheridan Le Fanu story. In the aimless sequel, *Lust For a Vampire* (1970), there was more sex than horror. Ingrid Pitt, star of *The Vampire Lovers*, was also seen bathing in virgins' blood in the title role of the gloomy *Countess Dracula* (1970).

In 1971 E.M.I. produced *Percy*, the comedy about a penis transplant; it was a theme that would have been unthinkable even two years earlier. Purely because they were produced by Columbia, the *Confessions* series, starring Robin Askwith, which thrived from 1974 to 1977, managed to attract character actors like Richard Wattis, Irene Handl and Doris Hare, players who normally would have scoffed at the idea of appearing in a sex film.

Pretty soon, however, many of their colleagues were taking part in even more disreputable examples of the genre, and there were often distinguished names on the other side of the camera. As early as 1965 Compton Bennett, director of the classic Forties weepie *The Seventh Veil*, had turned in *How to Undress in Public Without Undue Embarrassment*. Later veteran comedy writer-director Val Guest directed *Au Pair Girls* (1972) and *Confessions of a*

The Lovers' Guide 2: sex in the Nineties

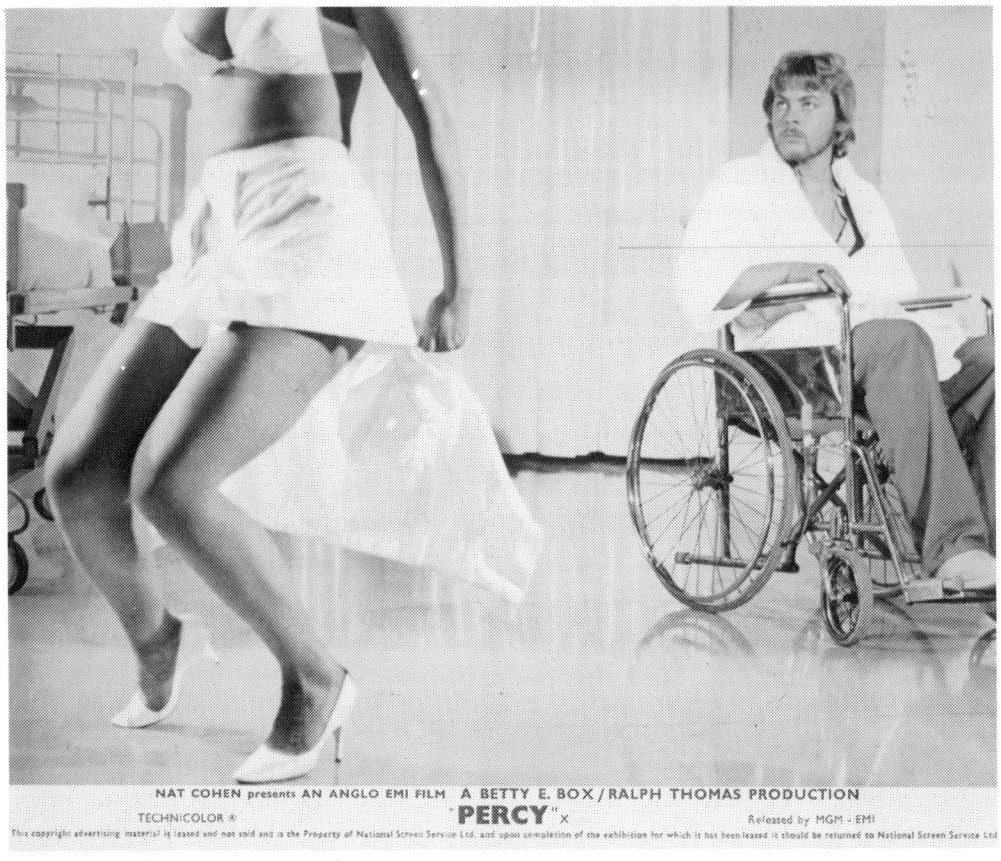

More sex therapy: Hywel Bennett in *Percy*

Clean Justine: Koo Stark in *Cruel Passion*

Window Cleaner (1974), while *Sex Play* (1975) was the work of American science-fiction king Jack Arnold. Jonathan Demme, who was to win an Oscar in 1991 for *The Silence of the Lambs*, was signed to direct *Secrets of a Door to Door Salesman* (1973), fired after a few days and replaced by Wolf *(Village of the Damned)* Rilla. (Demme's work still survives in the film behind the main titles.)

By the mid-Seventies there were some truly extraordinary figures dabbling in British sex films for fun and profit. The most aristocratic was undoubtedly the Earl of Pembroke, who used his professional name, Henry Herbert, to direct the appropriately genteel *Emily* (1976), supposedly Britain's answer to *Emmanuelle*. The film was not a success and nor was its much-publicised star Koo Stark. She went on to play Justine in *Cruel Passion* (1977), based on the writings of the Marquis de Sade, but eventually made her name not as an actress but as the consort of H.R.H. Prince Andrew. The Earl is now an established television director, with many series episodes (*Shoestring, Bergerac, King and Castle, The Saint, Moon and Son*) behind him.

In 1974 it was revealed that "Elton Hawke", who had been credited as the writer-producer of *Clinic Xclusive* (1971), a not uninteresting sex drama, was in fact a pseudonym masking the surprising collaboration between soap opera scriptwriter Hazel Adair and wrestling commentator Kent Walton. The odd couple - whose other films included *Can You Keep It Up For a Week?* (1974), probably the most famous sex film title of the Seventies - subsequently came clean in 1975 on the BBC2 programme *Man Alive*, which purported to disclose the "bare facts" about the British sexploitation business.

The critics were greatly amused by the programme (which was a pack of lies, and I should know because I was among those interviewed and told most of them), but the industry was even more amused when, within weeks of the programme being aired, its director, James Kenelm Clarke, began making sex films himself.

All three of them - *Exposé, Hardcore* and *Let's Get Laid!* - starred Fiona Richmond, then Britain's most uninhibited sex queen, who had attracted a large following from her work for sex impresario Paul Raymond. In most other countries the movies would have brought Fiona Richmond international stardom, but, clumsily miscast in a typically British fashion, she found instead that her career was grinding to a halt. Fortunately she was able to fall back on her intellectual skills and for a while she was in demand as a TV pundit.

Kenelm Clarke quit sex movies to produce middle-of-the-road entertainment such as *The 39 Steps* and *The Music Machine*, but he had one last stab at exploitation when he produced *Paul Raymond's Erotica* (1980), a film about Miss Richmond's former employer.

Far too late in the day, British producers got round to filming a couple of the pulp novels of former actress Jackie Collins. At odds with the dozens of disco hits on the soundtracks, the plots of *The Stud* (1978) and its sequel *The Bitch* (1979) were ludicrously behind the times. But the films did succeed in reactivating the stagnant career of their star, Joan Collins (sister of the authoress), who appeared coyly topless in *The Stud*. She was immediately summoned back to Hollywood, where she created a far more enduring bitch in TV's *Dynasty*.

Brother and sister team Malcolm and Adrienne Fancey, sexploitation veterans who had made a killing by snapping up the British distribution rights of the French film *Emmanuelle*, miscalculated with their 1979 film of another dated Jackie Collins novel, *The World Is Full of Married Men*. An audacious soap opera with typically unstimulating British sex film trimmings, it was a clinker.

British sex film production dwindled to one or two films a year in the late Seventies and ceased almost completely in 1981. The reasons for this shutdown were manifold. Foreign hardcore pornography, freely available in cinema clubs or on videotape for home viewing, stole the "raincoat trade" that had thrilled to the soft-core frolics of the British sex film for twenty years.

Inflation had rendered the low-cost production an impossibility. The days of the £50,000 budget recouped within eighteen months were gone, and the final straw came in 1980 when the newly-elected Conservative Government decided to end the concessionary subsidising of low-budget films. These factors also have to be weighed against the general decline of the British film industry - the loss of talent to other countries, the disappearance of the journeyman technician, the closure of cinemas.

During the dying days of the business, sex films could be produced only by an independently wealthy movie fan. This man was David Sullivan, the last tycoon of sexploitation and its youngest practitioner. Born in Cardiff in 1945, and described by even the radical *City Limits* magazine as "personable and schoolboyish", he reached his exalted position as Britain's highest-paid company director (£325,000 per annum) by graft and, by some people's definition, corruption.

University educated (he was an economics graduate from Queen Mary College), he began work in an advertising agency, but felt he could put his talents as a photographer to better use. "I'd read something about Bob Guccione starting by selling pictures to *Reveille*," he said, "and so I thought I'd do the same thing."

Sullivan progressed quickly from contributing to other people's magazines to publishing his own. Almost from the beginning, the Sullivan magazines (*Park Lane*, *Whitehouse*, *Playbirds*, etc.) broke new ground with their "spread shots". By the standards of the early Seventies, these were clearly indecent, but Sullivan invariably avoided obscenity charges with the defence that such pictures were sexually therapeutic.

Classic coupling: Edward Craven Walker's table lamp in the most famous British sex film of the Seventies

Tragic coupling: Alan Lake and Mary Millington in *Confessions from the David Galaxy Affair*

Shock value alone, however, could not have been marketed for any length of time, and the success of Sullivan's publications was due to the more enduring appeal of a model named Mary Millington.

Mary Millington was very much the Pamela Green of the Seventies. She had the quality of a sexpot-next-door with the additional bonus that her public image was that of an insatiable libertine. This was not in fact a million miles from the truth. A nude model since she left school, she had already performed in blue movies before meeting Sullivan in 1974. Later she was to become an expensive prostitute.

Having amassed a sizeable fortune from his magazines, his mail order business and a chain of sex shops, Sullivan decided, in the tradition of William Randolph Hearst, to turn Mary into a movie star. In 1977 he accepted the script *Come Play with Me* from Pamela Green's Svengali, Harrison Marks, and since Mary could not act, she was given a small supporting role.

It is a source of continuing amazement that *Come Play with Me* ran in London for four years. "It is not the best movie ever made," said producer Sullivan in a masterpiece of understatement. One is left with the inevitable conclusion that, despite her seemingly insignificant contribution, it was Mary Millington herself who was solely responsible for the film's popularity. However briefly it was on view, her genuine little-girl-lost charm captivated her audience. But, like Monroe, this was to be her downfall.

Sullivan quickly starred her in three more films - *The Playbirds, Confessions from the David Galaxy Affair* and *Queen of the Blues*. They were preposterously bad, but failed to dim Mary Millington's appeal. There were plans for further Millington movies, but in August, 1979, she killed herself in a fit of depression and loneliness. As a mark of unprecedented respect, London's sex cinemas closed for a day. And although he was castigated for sensationalism, Sullivan displayed a touching sincerity in his tribute to her, *Mary Millington's True Blue Confessions* (1980), a biopic which not even the BBC could have bettered.

Sullivan went on to produce *Emmanuelle in Soho* (1981), which had been intended as a vehicle for his late star. Her role was taken by newcomer "Randy" Mandy Miller (quite definitely not the child star of the same name.) On 13th May, 1982, David Sullivan was found guilty of living on the immoral earnings of prostitutes, a charge (which he denied) dating back to 1979. He was jailed for nine months and ordered to pay £10,000 costs.

"People are extremely jealous of success, particularly in the sex industry," Sullivan complained on his release in 1983. "If you make it in any other field, you get the Queen's Award for Industry. You make it in our industry, they send you to prison." Uninterested in producing further films, and temporarily unable, because of his conviction, to win a sex shop licence, Sullivan extended his publishing empire, and never looked back. His current position

Former veterinary nurse Mary Millington retained her devotion to animals: she and her companion were in *The Playbirds*

Bill Kerr too close for comfort in *Girls Come First*

Linda Hayden seeks closer contact with Fiona Richmond in *Exposé*

as Britain's richest press baron makes him the most visible, the most influential and, without doubt, the richest of the film-makers who contributed to a quarter of a century of British sexploitation.

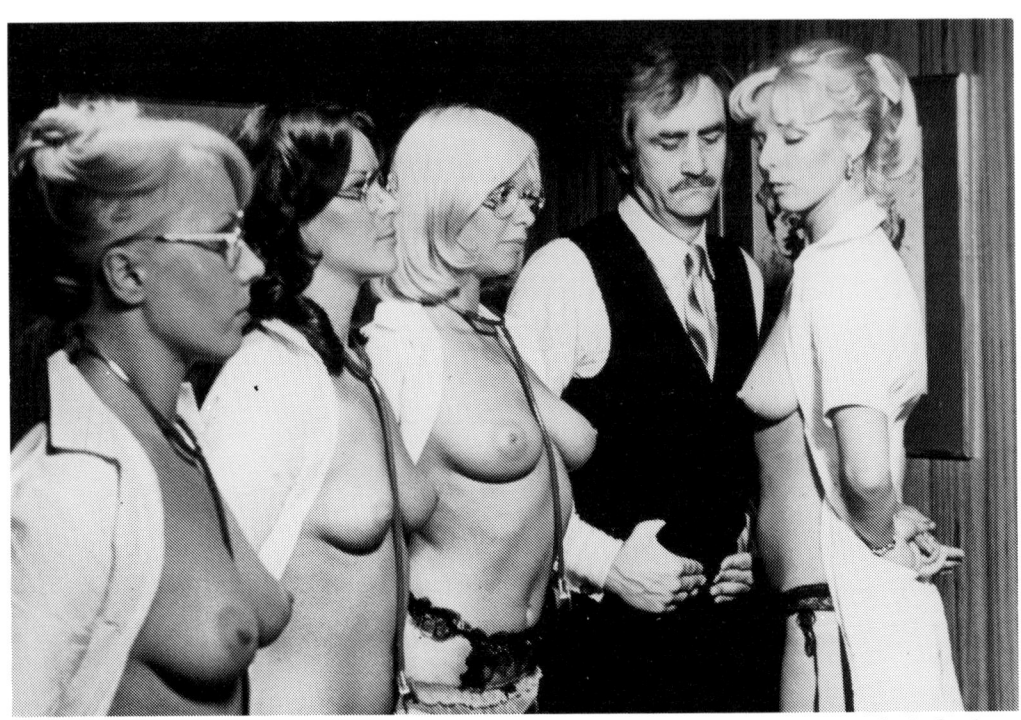

After appearing in *I'm Not Feeling Myself Tonight!*, James Booth left the country

He's behind you: Sally Faulkner and Barry Andrews in *I'm Not Feeling Myself Tonight!*

Chapter 5: "The Aftermath"

It was the Conservatives who were directly responsible for the death of the British sex film industry. Government policy discouraged production of the films, while the Tory-led Westminster City Council systematically purged Soho of its cinema clubs (along with its striptease theatres, peep shows, dirty bookshops, massage parlours and all other public outlets for the "vice trade"). Later the Video Recordings Act of 1984 successfully curbed the depiction of sex (and violence) in the new medium.

The likelihood, however, is that the sex film would have died no matter which political party had been in power. By the late Seventies it was clear that soft porn was on its last legs. Inflation and depleted audiences had turned the once safe bet into a risky investment, and its lack of appeal to young film-makers put paid to any hopes for a new lease of life.

In 1980 the Government merely delivered the *coup de grâce* by withdrawing the Eady fund used to subsidise British film production. One day, it is rumoured, somebody in authority actually took the trouble to check what kind of film public money was being used to promote, and cut off the funding there and then.

Surprisingly, public opinion played no small part in the purification of Soho, birth-place of the sex film in the Fifties. A place of ill-repute for centuries, Soho also possessed great cosmopolitan character zealously protected by its residents; and when the porn merchants began buying up restaurants, delicatessens and craft shops to house their garishly advertised operations, it was not just the religious extremists of the Festival of Light who protested, but more rational organisations such as the thousand-strong Soho Society, chaired by Leslie Hardcastle, later to found London's Museum of the Moving Image.

In 1975 the Society told the press that, in recent months, Soho had lost 25 corner shops and small family businesses to sex traders. The Society voted unanimously to press Westminster City Council for action. "This is not a moral issue," claimed Society spokesman Stephen Fry (not the actor-writer of the same name). "It is a question of self-preservation."

The Society had a staunch ally in Bernard Brook-Partridge, vociferous chairman of the Greater London Council's Public Services and Safety Committee, who stated openly "We are gunning for these people - by legal means of course."

Legally the authorities were in fact over a barrel, and particularly so with regard to the cinema clubs, which brazenly screened "HARD CORE PORN!", but on private premises to members only (and therefore, apparently, within the law). In 1977 the Association of Cinema Clubs agreed to moderate advertising displays visible to passers-by, but this uncharacteristic self-abnegation was short-lived, and the pictures of semi-naked porn starlets soon crept back into the cinema windows.

Uncertain of the extent of their own powers, the Obscene Publications Squad of the Metropolitan Police were reduced to the level of characters in a comic opera. Countless man-hours were wasted by planting policemen in clubs in the hope that they would find members of the audience masturbating. Such a victory would usually ensure the manager's conviction of running a disorderly house.

Otherwise policemen with nothing better to do raided cinemas and confiscated films, sometimes returning to the same premises two or three times a day. To John Lindsay, who opened the Taboo, Britain's first hard core cinema, in 1975, these raids were nothing more than a minor irritation. He told the *Daily Telegraph* in 1978: "Our customers simply stay where they are and wait for the raid to finish. We guarantee to re-open again in thirty minutes anyway. We have an unlimited stock of films."

The legal confusion reached the height of absurdity in 1981 when a judge criticised the police for trying to enforce the law as they saw it. Finding cinema manager David Browlie not guilty, Judge Cassel remarked, "To repeatedly raid and take away similar films was a decision which, in effect, is an act of censorship. It is an attempt to put the man out of business."

The Report of the Williams Committee, published in 1979, concluded, in essence, that pornography does not tend to deprave or corrupt.* The pornbrokers took this as their *carte blanche* to carry on regardless. The following year it was estimated that Soho's smut empire now incorporated 163 premises, approximately ninety of which were completely illegal. Gone forever were Isow's kosher restaurant, the Epicerie Française and the fifty-year-old Hamburger deli.

In November, 1980, Bernard Brook-Partridge's second-in-command, Bryan Cassidy, gave the porn kings another timid warning: "If external displays outside clubs were toned down," he ventured, "we would not be so worried about what went on behind closed doors - so long as there are no fire hazards."

This implied that the Greater London Council was prepared to suffer Soho's sex industry as long as it played ball. Certainly its main concern was public safety rather than moral welfare. But Westminster City Council had had all the impertinence it could take from a bunch of petty gangsters (Mafia connections

---

* The report *Pornography: Impacts and Influences* was commissioned by the Home Office in 1990. According to its co-author, Dr Guy Cumberbatch, Head of the Communications Research Unit at Aston University, "The fact that pornography causes crime is very difficult to support from the evidence." Home Secretary Kenneth Baker nevertheless found the Report "curiously inconclusive."

Sue Longhurst in Jonathan Demme's first film

Once more with feeling: Stanley Long directs Suzy Kendall and Christopher Neil in *Adventures of a Private Eye*

Sex in the suburbs: Sybilla Kay and Joan Alcorn in *Monique*

Another bargain from K-Tel: David Warbeck and Gloria Walker in *The Sex Thief*

were hinted at). Councillors had begun influencing M.P.s to take steps towards wiping this scum from the face of Soho.

At the end of 1981 the first of a series of draconian legislations was instigated. Shops whose stock included in excess of five per cent of naughty books, marital aids and other goods of a sexual nature were henceforth required to be licenced annually under a local byelaw. The Indecent Displays (Control) Act, introduced by Timothy Sainsbury, Conservative M.P. for Hove, became law, carrying with it a two year prison sentence for transgressors. In 1982 the Cinematograph Amendment Act required all sex cinemas to be licenced annually; Westminster City Council could refuse a licence if the premises were to be used for a purpose other than that for which planning permission had been given, or merely if the trade conducted would "damage the character of Soho."

Immediately the porn barons fell like ninepins. Early in 1982 Westminster City Council heard 29 appeals against enforcement and dismissed them all. At the end of the year Thomas Hayes, owner of the Exciting, Paradise and Queens cinemas, claimed that he was bankrupt. "In seven years [the police] raided my cinemas over three hundred times," he moaned before emigrating to Spain. In 1983 Erroll Thomas was fined £12,500 for operating a cinema without a licence, and John Lindsay was jailed for exhibiting obscene films. In 1984 five members of the Holloway family, former owners of the Astral cinema, were jailed for sending obscene materials through the post.

The Video Recordings Act, passed in 1984 in response to the previous year's "video nasty" furore, gave the British Board of Film Classification legal powers for the first time since the Board was established in 1913. The Act forbade the sale or hire of any pre-recorded video-cassette that had not been passed by the Board, and required soft core sex tapes, with the new "18R" certificate, to be sold only in licenced sex shops. A dealer caught offering uncertificated tapes could be fined £20,000 for each title sold. Anyone caught handling a banned tape faced the possibility of a prison sentence of up to three years, a fate which was to befall David Grant.

For several years following the clampdown, the most cunning of the pornbrokers found ways of skirting the law and staying in business. Sex shops masqueraded as erotic clothing stores or filled their shelves with 95% junk, while porn cinemas clung to survival with "music and dancing" licences. In 1986 *The Times* reported that there were still sixty illegal sex emporia operating in Soho. But their days were numbered.

In June, 1986, the General Powers Act gave Westminster City Council a kind of autocracy over Soho. In future, announced Peter Hartley, chairman of the Environment Committee, the Council would grant only ten licences per annum to sex traders, all of whom must be "responsible businessmen with no criminal record." By 1987 Soho's fleshpots had been reduced to five sex shops, three striptease theatres (including the Raymond Revuebar and Sunset Strip, two survivors from the Fifties) and two cinemas showing cut-down hard core films from the U.S.

Soho today is an increasingly chic enclave of advertising agencies, video companies and exotic restaurants. Since 1986 property values have soared and the soubriquet "Sohemian" has been coined. Ironically, however, Soho's richest property tycoon, controlling eight companies occupying fourteen buildings, is none other than Paul Raymond, he of the Revuebar. Whatever skill Raymond possessed, that which enabled him to see off virtually every Soho rival over five decades, has amassed him a personal fortune said to be in the region of £35 million.

The official line, handed to journalists at the time of going to press, is that hard core pornography no longer exists in Britain. Perhaps this is true of the now pristine borough of Westminster. But throughout the country, imported Danish magazines (notably the *Color Climax* series) are readily available from under the counter, and only a few miles north of Soho, in neighbouring Islington, two hard core cinemas have somehow eluded the porno pogrom. Others are known to exist in Birmingham and Manchester.

The only establishment to have been reconnoitred personally by the author (and his publisher) is a hole in the wall behind Kings Cross station. In a poky basement, nevertheless well served by illuminated exit signs, a cross-section of well-behaved punters, with and without raincoats, watches uncensored video tapes from Holland, Germany and the U.S. The programme is advertised nowhere, yet it is apparently common knowledge that it changes every Monday.

Although it is shocking to stumble across such an outlaw enterprise in supposedly porn-free Britain, it would be even harder to believe that anyone would ever go to the trouble of having such an insignificant little business closed down.

From 1982, when the sex film ceased to exist, to the present day, British cinema has been pretty much unsullied by sex in any form. In 1985, when the death of Rock Hudson pushed AIDS hysteria to its height, and actresses were said to be refusing to kiss their leading men, it seemed as though even screen romance, let alone unsimulated sexual intercourse, may become a thing of the past.

But the Nineties have brought a greater understanding of the nature of the disease and, with it, the international porn film industry has recovered its original momentum. Major productions, shot on 35mm with budgets of $150,000, are not uncommon and, as Russia, Poland, Hungary and other countries of the former Communist bloc open up to the adult film experience of the West, far greater expansion is predicted. "They cannot believe how good our quality is," boasts Hollywood distributor Todd L. Blatt.

The Nine Ages of Nakedness: the Stone Age - Harrison Marks-style

From the woman who gave us *Crossroads:* Neil Hallett and Françoise Pascal in *Keep It Up Downstairs*

Britain, however, has taken what can only be regarded as a long overdue retirement from the sex film arena she never should have entered. 1986 saw the last foreign soft porn movies booked into British cinemas. Starved for product, London's renowned Eros and Moulin cinemas closed their doors for the last time in 1985 and 1990 respectively.

Since 1982 less than a dozen British pictures have used sex as a central feature of their plots.Perhaps the re-make of *Fanny Hill* (1983), directed by sex film veteran Gerry O'Hara, and *Screw Loose* (1984), featuring a character named Anita Blackhouse, were the last films displaying direct lineage with the cheeky sex romps of the old school. Two later films used peculiarly British, true-life sex scandals as their themes: *Personal Services* (1987) was the unofficial biopic of South London brothel-keeper Cynthia Payne, and *Scandal* (1988) told the story of Christine Keeler and Mandy Rice-Davies, the prostitutes who brought down the Tory government in 1964.* *The Pleasure Principle* (1991), about a philandering journalist named Dick, was castigated by British critics for making no reference to AIDS.

Although videotape was first developed in the Fifties, feature films were not made available on video-cassette until 1972. Widespread domestic use of video, another nail in the coffin of the traditional British sex film, began in 1980. The home entertainment medium seemed tailor-made for the voyeur, who never could have been entirely at ease indulging his pleasure in the company of perhaps two or three hundred like-minded individuals. During the less crowded afternoon screenings at sex cinemas, the men would always sit as far as possible from each other.

Some of the earliest British sex tapes, particularly those of Michael Freeman, the porn pioneer from the Sixties, clung doggedly to narrative conventions that were already being jettisoned by rival companies. Freeman apparently thought highly of his tapes, or "videograms" as he called them, even offering them for sale at Cannes. But in fact the technical standard of his productions was staggeringly inept.

Between 1980-81 Freeman made around twenty hard core tapes, including *Adventures of Alison, More Adventures of Alison, French Lessons* and *Lady Victoria's Training,* all of which were more primitive than even the work of Arnold Louis Miller at his most impoverished. *Glass Table Orgy* (1981) has a fellation scene that takes up half the tape's running time. *Truth or Dare* (1981) has no script, no plot and virtually no editing or camera movement. It is almost as if the past ninety years of motion picture history had not existed. But it is

---

* In their book *Porn Gold* (1988), David Hebditch and Nick Anning claim that, prior to the Profumo affair, Christine Keeler appeared in a hard core porn film called *100% Lust,* directed by Ivor Cooke. (Mandy Rice-Davies became a straight actress in the Seventies. She appeared in *Dirty Linen,* the Tom Stoppard play inspired by the Profumo affair, and later in the film *Absolute Beginners* [1986]).

pathetically, charmingly, horribly, wonderfully English. At one point the heroine (Paula Meadows) pauses for breath during a sombre bout of fellatio and opines, "It was never like this in Basingstoke."

Freeman's *oeuvre* put him behind bars in 1982, but he gamely returned to the business in 1987 to front Puff Video, a company producing cut-down hard core and new soft core tapes including - not that they are worth searching out - *A Day with Sarah, Lolita James* and *Solitaire*. Puff Video is currently based in Holland.

The sex tape business as it evolved owed little allegiance to English heritage erotica, although, even into the Nineties, tapes were still issued bearing titles that only an Englishman could have dreamed up: *Sexy Secrets of the Kissogram Girls* (1985), *Jane and Janice Get Them Off* (1987), *Raunchy Randy Ravers* (1990).

Otherwise the ramshackle sex comedies of yesteryear and the Euro-style adult entertainment now on the video shelves are different breeds. Narrative is a thing of the past, and the little humour that exists, e.g. in Electric Blue's "Boobwoman" sketches, owes more to *The Comic Strip* than *Carry On Sergeant*. The cheapness and portability of video has also freed the performers from studio sets and bracing English seaside resorts and taken them to more glamorous foreign locations.

Remarkably - given the ever-watchful presence of the B.B.F.C. (the acronym now stands for British Board of Film Classification, but it remains a board of censorship) - there is also a far more diverse range of sexuality available to the home viewer than his cinemagoing predecessor. Sex shop browsers can choose from tapes devoted to Lesbians, transvestites, naturists, women with large breasts, female strippers, male strippers, amateur strippers, mud wrestlers, nude wrestlers, sex education, corporal punishment and even foot fetishism. And all, naturally, in the best possible taste.

From the dawn of the video age, the brand leader in the sex shops has been the *Electric Blue* label, originally sold by mail-order via advertisements in Paul Raymond's magazines *Men Only* and *Club International*, but now a familiar sight in high street stores. Three magazine-format (striptease, sketches, news items) tapes plus additional "specials" are issued each year. The *Electric Blue* house-style has been much emulated, but rarely successfully, and the label is currently the favourite in what amounts to a one-horse race. It is not unusual for selections from more than forty volumes of *Electric Blue* to comprise a shop's entire stock of British sex tapes.

The label had the good fortune to be launched (in September, 1979, by former *Penthouse* photographer Adam Cole) in a blaze of negative, but useful publicity. Since then Cole has maintained his media contacts and, it must be said, maintained a reasonable standard of production. He also claims to be in tune with the British punter's way of thinking. The average British male, he

The doctor will see you now: Venicia Day in *Can You Keep It Up for a Week?*

says, fantasises about the girl next door rather than the young, blonde, Californian centrefold. Tapes featuring viewers' nude wives ("Doreen from Dorking") are best-sellers.

Among the attractions in *Electric Blue No. 002* (1980) was a clip from Malcolm Leigh's *Games That Lovers Play* (1970) featuring Joanna Lumley with no clothes on (six years before she became a New Avenger). Apparently Miss Lumley had no objections to the exposé, but Diane Hart, a fully-clothed character actress in the same clip, claimed that she had been made an object of ridicule, and sued *Electric Blue*. Unexpectedly the Court found in her favour, and Cole deeply resents the "considerable sum of money" he was forced to pay her.

Electric Blue No. 003 (1981) was presented by Britt Ekland, who also filed a complaint, this time because her material was used without her permission in Cole's one-off big screen version, *Electric Blue - The Movie* (1981). The Ekland scenes had to be removed. In 1984 *Electric Blue Volumes 001-007* and *Nude Wives Special Parts 1 and 2* were found not obscene at Knightsbridge Crown Court. (The remainder of the *Electric Blue* volumes has been released without litigation).

In common with all other video-cassettes of the period, *Volumes 001-19* were uncertificated. In spite of this freedom, the sex content was merely explicit ("spread shots", masturbation, etc.), not hard core. *Volume 20* (1985), the first to be released, following the introduction of the Video Recordings Act, with an "18" certificate, was noticeably tame and set the parameters still observed to this day. Some of the uncertificated material has been cleaned up and re-released, somewhat dishonestly, as *The Best of Electric Blue.*

Like the sex films of yore, *Electric Blue* caters exclusively to the British market. This, needless to say, is not by choice; but, with the exception of a few foreign TV sales, soft core sex is now unsaleable in all major territories. Cole reckons that *Electric Blue* will run to a few more volumes, but worries about the inevitable day when hard core porn is beamed into Britain via satellite. He hopes to diversify by moving into feature films, and has two projects - one on Rasputin, the other a psychic thriller called *The Electric Man* - on the drawing board.

No sooner had *Electric Blue* burst on the scene in 1979 than rival companies rushed out their own tapes. Many were pale imitations of the video magazine concept, and one, *Top Secret* (1982), even duplicated the *Electric Blue* logo. *International Red Tape*, which ran to three volumes in 1981, was hosted by alternative comedian-cum-actor Keith Allen, and *Private Spy* (1982-84), an attempt at a video tabloid, was presented by all manner of quasi-celebrities including Reginald Bosanquet and John McVicar.

Female striptease has always been well represented on video. So venerable (it opened in 1958) that it is now part of the establishment, the Raymond

Nearly a superstar: Linzi Drew in *I Love Linzi*

Someone's got to do it: Britt Ekland presented *Electric Blue 003*

Revuebar produces the kind of lavish nude spectacular that can be found in any of the world's capital cities. *Electric Blue* recorded a typical Raymond show in 1982.

Of greater sociological interest is the British form of burlesque - low-grade strippers plus blue comics - fostered by pub culture. *The Great British Striptease* (1980), also transferred to film for cinema release, records a Blackpool striptease competition compèred by the notoriously racist comedian Bernard Manning. Su Pollard, later popular in TV's *Hi-de-Hi!*, can be seen scampering about, collecting discarded garments. Even earthier shows are the subjects of *Stag Night* and *Super Stagarama* (both 1981), examples of British night-life at its scuzziest. We will deal later with the subject of male striptease, a phenomenon of the Nineties.

The ubiquitous David Sullivan naturally moved swiftly into video, saturating the market with heavy-duty porn - including *Deep Wet Lust*, an enema tape - from 1980 until the censorship axe fell in 1984. It is a Sullivan tape, *Whitehouse Video Show No. 1*, which features a woman masturbating while watching her pet snake eat a rat, surely the most bizarre image in British porn. Sullivan was also behind four volumes of *The Rustler Connoisseur's Collection*, compilations of the Mistral range of hard core loops shot by glamour photographer turned pornographer Russell Gay. One movie, *Response*, starred the young Mary Millington.

Zeta, Sullivan's top model in the early days of his scandal sheet, the *Sunday Sport*, debuted on video in *Fantasy Manor* and later chaired *Zeta's Sexy Video Show*, an outrageous chat show tape with nude guests.

Zeta was one of very few stars whose name could be used to sell a sex tape. The most famous nude celebrities of the Eighties, Samantha Fox and Linda Lusardi, gained their fame through modelling and personal appearances, not video. To date video has failed to produce anyone of the stature of the cinema's Pamela Green and Mary Millington. The names of video's most popular performers are unlikely to be known outside the sex shop coterie.

Like Fiona Richmond, Pat Wynn has a journalistic background (she was an agony aunt for *Fiesta* magazine). An unusually mature performer, certainly in her forties and possibly even older, she has been seen in the *Bounce* series (1984-86), *Miss Adventures at Mega Boob Manor* (1987) and two volumes of *In with Auntie* (1989). By contrast performers do not come any younger than Bernice Outram who stirred moral outrage by shooting scenes from *Unbelievable Experience* (1989) on her sixteenth birthday.[*]

In addition to Pat Wynn, other well-endowed stars include Titanic Toni, Stacey Owen and the improbable Tina Small, whose reputed 84" bust is highly

---

[*] The Protection of Children Act, prohibiting those under the age of sixteen from participating in sex acts for films or any other medium, became law in 1978.

suspect. Also popular are page three girl Debee Ashby, who debuted in *Sexy Secrets of the Sex Therapist* (1987) and told the world of her affair with Tony Curtis; Janie Hamilton, seen in *King Arthur's Lady Returns* (1986) and *The Naughty Dreams of Miss Owen* (1987); Jackie Hunter, "sex sensation of the Eighties", in *The Initiants* (1988); and Marie Harper, who edited the *Electric Blue* magazine and was regularly teamed with Linzi Drew.

Linzi is the nearest to - but, by international standards, still light years from - a video superstar, not only a sex symbol, but a martyr for the cause. Yet another literary lion (she was the editor of *Penthouse* magazine), Linzi gained a cult following from modelling appearances in men's magazines and early *Electric Blue* tapes. She also played a sex film actress in *An American Werewolf in London* (1981) and a naked nun in Ken Russell's *The Lair of the White Worm* (1988).

In 1992 she was convicted of possession of pornography and imprisoned together with her partner, Lindsay Honey, a pop musician turned porn actor, who has worked for Michael Freeman and David Sullivan and who directed the almost criminally bad sex thriller *Death Shock* (1982). Liberated after serving two months of a four month sentence, Linzi appeared on late night television on the day of her release to plug a tape called *Members Only*.

Also imprisoned in 1991 (for selling "obscene" and uncertificated tapes) was Stephanie Anne Lloyd, transexual manager of Transformation, a chain of stores dealing in magazines, clothes and synthetic breasts for transvestites. One of the illegal tapes, *Female Domination* (1989), shows two secretaries taking revenge on their chauvinist boss by dressing him in women's clothes and then spanking him.

Although crudely made, the tape features neither sex nor frontal nudity and is as playfully harmless as a Sixties glamour movie. The corpsing and some of the improvised dialogue is even quite cherishable. Lloyd's company, T.M.C., now releases even milder tapes, e.g. *My Husband in Panties, Lesbian She-Males*, with B.B.F.C. approval.

Just as it has failed as a star-maker, so the sex tape industry has failed to attract much creative talent. Consequently the general standard of British sex tapes is lower than that of foreign counterparts. Productions on the *Electric Blue* label (mostly directed by Vic Marchant) and those of its main rival, a company known variously as Strand International, Piccadilly and Action Essential, are acceptable of their type. But recently three genres of tape have set new benchmarks for quality, some examples surpassing the production values of any sex subject shot on film or tape in Britain over the past 35 years. Two of the genres - naturism and sex education - are revivals of old favourites. The third - male striptease - is apparently an original.

There would appear to be no precedent for the male stripper prior to the Seventies. *The Rise and Fall of Ivor Dickie* (1977), a striptease documentary, includes an item on the eponymous Ivor, who strips at hen parties, for its novelty value.

The concept of muscular teams of male strippers performing for female audiences in clubs and theatres began in the U.S. in the Eighties with The Chippendales. A British version, The Dreamboys, was formed in 1989, and soon there were a dozen similar acts touring the country. Many were flashily and successfully taped, but it is claimed that *The London Knights* (1991) and *The London Knights 2* (1992) outsold other British tapes because the Knights take everything off. (Other teams, in common with female strippers of the Fifties, keep their G-strings on). Male striptease and magazines with male nudes such as *For Women* form part of the first widely successful attempt to market what has been categorised as female pornography. Developing alongside a complementary male interest in bodybuilding and exhibitionism, it would appear to have greater potential.

In 1987 naturism was retrieved as a subject for exploitation, not as surprising a development as it may seem. In the two decades since the movement was last considered newsworthy, many Britons had had personal experience of foreign nudist beaches. Now a topic to which they could relate could be treated without Fifties bashfulness.

Educating Julie, the first nudist picture for 24 years, and the first to be shot on video, was a vast improvement technically on most of the original nudies, but, rather charmingly, it respected the age-old traditions of the genre by using a plot in which an outsider is converted to the naturist ethos. The tape was used as a visual aid by the producers of the 1991 TV commercial for Danepak bacon.

Three more nudies - *Hitch-Hike, Perfect Exposure* and *Alison Over the Moon* - appeared in 1991, all directed by Charlie Simonds. The same year Rob Bayley directed *Streaker!*, a documentary, hosted by George Best (!), on the craze for running naked through public functions, which reached its zenith in 1974 (when Robert Opel streaked through the Oscar ceremony). It's highly unlikely, however, that the fad for small screen, peek-a-boo nudity will survive any longer than its original incarnation on the big screen.

Sex education was back with a vengeance in 1991, making British screen history in the process. *The Lovers' Guide*, which rocketed almost to the top of the video sales charts and remained in the listings for six months, covered much the same ground (how to make the most of your love life) as the instructional films of the Seventies, and even revived the mollifying convention of a "sexpert" (in this case Dr Andrew Stanway) talking to camera. But the tape used sexual imagery that would have had the producers of *Love Variations* clapped into irons.

For the first time in history the B.B.F.C. passed for adult exhibition unsimulated intercourse, oral sex and masturbation. It goes without saying that this material also entailed allowing the sight of an erect penis, but this was

60 minutes of adult entertainment:
Electric Blue 001

Gay sex video shocker: *The Gay Man's Guide to Safer Sex*

not a breakthrough. The British cinema's first erection had been seen in Derek Jarman's *Sebastiane* in 1976. (It belonged to Ken Hicks).

The rationale for the B.B.F.C.'s *volte-face* is disputed. It has been suggested that the Board is trying subtly to bring British censorship in line with that of the rest of Europe. But a Board spokesman claims that *The Lovers' Guide*, as opposed to hard core pornography, is "justified as being in the public good" under the terms of the Obscene Publications Act, 1959.

Shot on film, its attractive couples captured in pretty soft-focus by Peter Sinclair, who lit Stanley Long's three *Adventures* films (1975-78) and at least one piece of hard porn, *Body Love* (1976), *The Lovers' Guide* offered some of the most genuinely erotic moments ever created in a British sex movie - as well as some sensible advice. Perhaps the tape really was bought by couples who wanted to make the most of their love life. We may never know.

What could easily have been predicted was that the tape opened the floodgates for more of the same. The British contributions included *Making Love* (1991), the inevitable *The Lovers' Guide 2* (1992), and Penthouse Video's *Supervirility* (1992), which offered men tips on how to improve their love-making technique, and was helmed by the first British woman director in the field, Victoria Norwood.

Also released in 1992 was a tape whose motives were genuinely beyond reproach, *The Gay Man's Guide to Safer Sex*. Shot TV documentary-style with raunchy sex scenes (one in the shower looking as though it was inspired by *Flashdance*), it promoted a forcefully positive image of gay life and cleared up many misconceptions about HIV and AIDS to counteract tabloid scaremongering. *En passant* it also broke down even more censorship barriers (although unsimulated oral and anal sex were nowhere near as upfront as sexual activity in the heterosexual primers).

Sex film genres may well continue to come and go as gaps appear in the market, but we must resign ourselves to the fact that the British sex film *per se* is gone forever. In the U.S. the nudies and nudie-cuties produced between 1958-1969 are now being tracked down - a tough task, we're told - and re-issued on video. But in this country the much more restricted video industry could not accommodate such esoteric titles. The films will never be seen again.

For those who care to dig deeper, however, the influence of the British sex film can be detected in many incongruous contexts. The Sex Pistols' creator, Malcolm McLaren, is obviously a student of the British sex comedy; he set one scene of *The Great Rock 'n' Roll Swindle* in London's Moulin cinema and had members of the audience played by Mary Millington and *Carry On* stalwart Liz Fraser.

American director Paul Morrissey is a self-confessed *Carry On* fan; when he came to England to make *The Hound of the Baskervilles*, he cast Kenneth

Full circle: Danepak TV commercial 1991

Not guilty: Electric Blue's Steve Hughes, Vic Marchant and Adam Cole celebrate outside Knightsbridge Crown Court, 1984

Williams as Sir Henry Baskerville. And a particularly delightful *hommage* occurs in John Landis' *An American Werewolf in London* in which David Naughton turns into a werewolf while watching a British sex film, starring Linzi Drew, in the Eros cinema, Piccadilly Circus.

Most recently the aforementioned Danepak commercial featured two naked couples in a naturist reserve cooking and eating the low-fat bacon while a variety of props (most memorably a Thermos flask) concealed their private parts. Although directly inspired by a TV sketch starring comedians Hale and Pace, this in turn was a parody of the nudies of antiquity. As if to prove the immutability of the British character, the majority of viewers found the commercial uproarious, while 24 prudes complained to the Independent Television Commission. (The complaints were rejected and the nudists are due to appear in another Danepak commercial at the end of 1992).

From a conversation with the commercial's writer, Stephen Henry, an even more intriguing fact emerges. Apparently the two male nudists had been allowed freedom of movement by the I.T.C., but the Commission insisted that the two women must remain immobile. This was because a moving, naked woman on prime-time television was unacceptably exploitative.

With that momentous decision, the years fell away and we were transported back before video porn, before naughty knickers and saucy schoolgirls at the local Odeon, before Pamela Green flickered to black and white life on the bedroom wall, and even before the word "virgin" could be spoken in a film, to World War II, a time when the showgirls at the Windmill theatre were permitted to appear nude as long as they didn't move.

Glib as it may sound, the wheel really did appear to have turned full circle.

APPENDIX

The Main Instigators and What Became of Them

I have managed to track down all the characters in this book with the exception of some of the starlets. Throughout the Seventies, nurses, housewives, girlfriends and schoolgirls were played by a veritable repertory company of young actresses who would strip at the drop of a pun. Despite limited acting ability, most had at least one shot at playing a lead. Their careers ended with the sex film business itself, and one can safely assume that the majority opted for marriage and early retirement. (The author would be happy to receive definite confirmation).

HAZEL ADAIR

Hazel Adair is assured a place in television history as the creator (with Peter Ling) of the most loved/hated soap opera of all time, *Crossroads*. But her comparably significant contribution to sex films should not be overlooked. A television writer from 1950, she contributed to the pioneer soaps *Emergency - Ward 10* and *Compact*. She showed an early aptitude for lowbrow humour by scripting the *Carry On*-styled *Dentist on the Job* (1961). In 1970 she and Kent Walton formed Pyramid Films, adopting the joint pseudonym "Elton Hawke" to produce *Clinic Xclusive* (1971) and *Can You Keep It Up For a Week?* (1974). After coming out of the closet, Miss Adair wrote and produced *Keep It Up Downstairs* (1976) under her own name. Her last major credit (producer/2nd unit director) was for the action picture *Game For Vultures* (1979). Since then she claims to have written *Miss Candida* (1980) and *Valley of the Vines* (1981), two series for German television, and written and produced *Sweeter Than Wine* (1988) and *Love Me, Leave Me* (1989), two romantic dramas unseen in Britain. She is now developing a soap opera and a weekly series for television, and plans to produce a film of Graham Greene's novel *A Burnt-Out Case* and an action adventure, *Masai*, to be shot in Kenya.

MICHAEL ARMSTRONG

Michael Armstrong's natural inclination is towards classical drama, but he earned his bread and butter as a jack-of-all-trades in exploitation pictures from the late Sixties onwards. A former actor, RADA trained, he learned how to direct films by directing films, firstly a short for Negus-Fancey, *The Image*

(1969), introducing David Bowie, then a feature for Tony Tenser, *The Haunted House of Horror* (1989). "The first day I walked on to the set," Armstrong admits, "I looked through the wrong end of the camera." In 1970 he went to Germany to direct his last film to date, *Mark of the Devil*, "ninety minutes of solid violence", still banned in Britain. Armstrong's long partnership with writer-producer Tudor Gates began in 1973 when he wrote and appeared in Gates' *The Sex Thief*, a resourceful sex comedy directed by Martin Campbell. The following year Armstrong began another long association, this time with Stanley Long, who produced *Eskimo Nell*, directed by Campbell and written by Armstrong as a vendetta against British low-budget film-making. In it Armstrong plays himself, a director exploited by unsavoury producers. Armstrong was involved in Long's *Adventures* trilogy (1976-78) and also wrote Long's sex education drama *It Could Happen to You* (1976) and *The Black Panther* (1977), the true story of Donald Neilson, who kidnapped and murdered 15-year-old Lesley Whittle in 1975. For Pete Walker he wrote the script of the unfilmed Sex Pistols movie *A Star Is Dead* (1978). At the end of the Seventies he became involved with a company called Maiden Music, which collapsed in 1981 leaving a stockpile of still-born Armstrong projects. They included a series of puppet films and a multi-million dollar live action/cartoon combination called *The Enchanted Orchestra*. Armstrong went on to script episodes of *The Professionals* and *Shoestring* and between 1982-83 wrote three fantasy shorts, directed by Long, which were later linked and issued on video as *Scream Time*. In 1983 he wrote Pete Walker's last film to date, *House of the Long Shadows*. The following year he went to Los Angeles and stayed. He failed to find finance for a feature film called *Orphanage*. Instead he wrote unfilmed screenplays for producer Sandy Howard and wrote and directed a stage musical called *My Jewish Vampire*. In 1989 he was tempted to Paris to write three more screenplays (all unfilmed). He returned to England in somewhat reduced circumstances and was obliged to serve behind the bar at the Top Rank club in Reading. Back on his feet in 1990, he wrote and directed the Christopher Lee prologue added to the video re-issue of the silent *The Phantom of the Opera*. In 1991 he produced Tudor Gates' play *The Kidnap Game* at the Theatre Royal, Windsor. In his spare time he has always taught drama and now runs his own drama school, the Armstrong Arts Academy, whose debut production, *The Illustrated Games People Play*, ran for a fortnight in London in 1992.

ROBIN ASKWITH

After making his film debut as a schoolboy in *If....* (1968), Robin Askwith spent the rest of his career as the archetypal cheeky young buck, forever ogling topless birds and trying to get his leg over. He worked three times for Pete

Walker - in *Cool It Carol!* (1970), *The Four Dimensions of Greta* and *The Flesh and Blood Show* (both 1972) - and in 1973 did his stuff in another notable trio, *Carry On Girls*, *No Sex Please - We're British* and Antony Balch's *Horror Hospital*. But it was as Timmy Lea in the four *Confessions* films (1974-77) that he became a British sex film icon. His final appearance in the genre was the title role (Gordon Laid) in *Let's Get Laid!* (1977) co-starring Fiona Richmond. But he continued playing the same kind of roles on stage, in *Further Confessions of a Window Cleaner* (1978), *Who Goes Bare* (1979) and other saucy farces. Long out of the public eye in Britain, he has spent recent years in Australia and New Zealand, directing and starring in tours of *Run For Your Wife* and *One for the Road*.

NICOLA AUSTINE
A pretty little blonde starlet, one of the busiest during the Seventies. She had a leading role in *Suburban Wives* (1971) and was also in *Secrets of Sex* (1969), *Up Pompeii* and *Not Tonight Darling!* (both 1971), *The Love Box* and *Commuter Husbands* (1972), *On the Game* (1973), *Vampira* (1974), *Come Play with Me* (1977), *What's Up Superdoc* (1978), *The World Is Full of Married Men* and *Queen of the Blues* (both 1979), *Sex with the Stars* (1980) and *Nutcracker* (1982).

ANTONY BALCH
For more than ten years Wardour Street's most flamboyant and daring - and good looking - distributor, Antony Balch was ahead of his time in many respects, but specifically in that he ignored spurious divisions between "good" and "bad" films. He programmed two London cinemas, the Times in Baker Street and the Jacey in Piccadilly, with classics, trash and trash classics, and tried, sometimes unsuccessfully, to make a quick buck by distributing foreign sex films. His skill at re-titling, always done tongue-in-cheek, was renowned: *Juliette de Sade* (1969) became *Heterosexual* in the hope that some might assume this to be an exciting new sexual deviation. He delighted in baiting censors, infuriating critics and generally causing trouble. Involved in film production from 1954, he was originally a production assistant, then an editor and director, for shorts and commercials. For his short film, *Towers Open Fire* (1963), a visual approximation of William Burroughs' literary style, Balch filmed himself masturbating. He completed only two features, *Secrets of Sex* (1969) and *Horror Hospital* (1973). The uncut version of *Secrets of Sex*, released on video in some countries as *Bizarre*, is worth tracking down. Balch died of cancer on 6th April, 1980, at the age of 43. One of his obituaries called him "an abominable showman".

ANNA BERGMAN
No other starlet came to British sex films with a more impressive pedigree than Anna Bergman: the Swedish sexpot is Ingmar Bergman's daughter. A model in London from 1967, she played the title role in *Penelope Pulls It Off* (1975) and secondary roles in *Adventures of a Taxi Driver* (1975), *Intimate Games* (1976), *Come Play with Me* and *The Wild Geese* (both 1977), *What's Up Superdoc* (1978), *Licensed to Love and Kill* (1979) and *Nutcracker* (1982). She also worked in Denmark in *Agent 69* (1977) and *Emmanuelle in Denmark* (1986). Apparently she still lives in London.

MINAH BIRD
The only major black starlet in British sex films, Minah Bird also played bits in mainstream movies and was regularly on TV in the Seventies. She had a leading role in *Layout for 5 Models* (1972). Her other films were *Up Pompeii* (1971), *The Four Dimensions of Greta* and *The Love Box* (both 1972), *Percy's Progress* (1974), *Alfie Darling* (1975), *The Stud* (1978) and *The London Connection* (1979).

TIM BLACKSTONE
Ebullient sex film actor, usually cast as a stud in the Seventies. He was in *The Hot Girls* and *All I Want Is You... and You... and You* (both 1974), *Sex Express* and *I'm Not Feeling Myself Tonight!* (both 1975), *Under the Bed* (1976) and *Emmanuelle in Soho* (1981).

JULIA BOND
Average-looking starlet in *Ups and Downs of a Handyman* (1975), *The Office Party* and *Sextet* (both 1976), *What's Up Nurse* and *Confessions from a Holiday Camp* (both 1977) and also the stage comedy *Come into My Bed* (1976).

SUE BOND
Sue Bond was a buxom, blonde actress usually in comedy roles in films and on TV. She starred in *The Yes Girls* (1972) and was also in *Secrets of Sex* (1969), *Freelance* (1970), *White Cargo* (1973), *The Best of Benny Hill* (1974), *Come Play with Me* (1977) and *George and Mildred* (1980). Recently she has been attempting a new career as a singer.

JOHN BOWN

John Bown was an actor whose chief claim to fame was playing a Thal in *Dr Who and the Daleks* (1965). With no film-making experience behind him, he directed an eleven minute short, *Northwest Confidential*, on a budget of £1,200. This was chosen to support *Wonderwall*, one of the opening attractions at the Cinecenta, London's first multi-screen cinema, in 1967. Bown then wrote the screenplay for *Monique*, a vehicle for his wife, Sibylla Kay, and took it to Tony Tenser, who eventually agreed to allow Bown to direct it. Probably the first British film to deal frankly with Lesbianism and a *ménage-à-trois*, *Monique* (1969) is almost certainly the most accomplished British sex drama. It fared well in Britain and the U.S., but was to be Bown's only feature film as a director. He wanted his next project to be a thriller, *Hey, You!*, but could not find the backing for it. He resumed acting, joining the cast of the TV series *Doomwatch* (1971), and taking small roles in the films *Vampire Circus* (1971) and *Fear in the Night* (1972). From 1976-79 he was a member of the Royal Shakespeare Company. Now semi-retired, he paints and writes plays.

AVA CADELL

Pert, squeaky-voiced and well-endowed Ava Cadell came to Britain from Hungary and worked as a model and dancer. Her first film appearances were for John Lindsay. She was credited as Eva Chatt in *The Hot Girls* (1974) and changed her name for *Confessions of a Sex Maniac* (1974), *Ups and Downs of a Handyman* (1975) and *Outer Touch* and *The Golden Lady* (both 1979). In 1980 she and her husband, Andrew Martin-Smith, went to Florida to open a restaurant. They moved on to Los Angeles, where Ava has been in episodes of *Dallas*, *The Fall Guy* and *Matt Houston*.

MARTIN CAMPBELL

Martin Campbell was one of only two directors (the other being Robert Hartford-Davis) able to use British exploitation pictures as a springboard to Hollywood. He revealed above-average ability in his first film, *The Sex Thief* (1973), which was released in the U.S., with interpolated hard core footage, as *Her Family Jewels*. Next came an excellent satire, *Eskimo Nell* (1974), wittily scripted by Michael Armstrong and an invaluable record of the prevailing conditions in the soft core industry. (Benny U. Murdoch, head of B.U.M. Productions, is a caricature of Tony Tenser). After a sad aberration, *Three For All* (1974), a failed attempt to re-capture the jollity of the Cliff Richard musicals of the Sixties, Campbell was the production supervisor of Tudor Gates' *Intimate Games* (1976) and associate producer of *Scum* (1977) before moving into television. Here he directed episodes of *Minder*, *Shoestring*, *The Profes-*

sionals, Bergerac and *Muck and Brass* among others before being awarded two major projects, the mini-series *Edge of Darkness* (1985) and the TV movie *Frankie and Johnnie* (1986). Not surprisingly, *Criminal Law* (1989), with Gary Oldman and Kevin Bacon, was described as Campbell's first feature film. He followed it with *Defenseless* (1991), with Barbara Hershey, and a TV movie *Cast a Deadly Spell* (1991).

HEATHER DEELEY

One of the casualties of British sex films, Heather Deeley had a meteoric career lasting two years, was washed up at the age of 21, and is now completely forgotten. Her big year was 1975, when she appeared in six films. There were minor roles in *Erotic Inferno, Pink Orgasm, Girls Come First, I'm Not Feeling Myself Tonight!* and *Secrets of a Superstud*, plus her only lead in Derek Ford's *Sex Express* a.k.a. *Diversions*. The same year she was hailed as "Britain's new sex symbol." But she was to make only two more, fleeting, appearances in *Intimate Games* (1976) and *Hardcore* (1977). By this time her personal habits, encouraged by a new boyfriend, had made her unreliable. She showed no interest in further offers of work and disappeared. Some months later she was discovered working in a Soho peep show. Her present whereabouts are unknown.

FELICITY DEVONSHIRE

A very popular starlet and not a bad actress, "Fluff", as she was known to all, played quite a few leads and went to Italy to star in *Blue Belle* (1975). She was also the star of her last film, *What's Up Nurse* (1977), in which she greatly impressed director Derek Ford by agreeing to be thrown into the North Sea - twice - in November. Her other films were *Sex and the Other Woman* and *The Four Dimensions of Greta* (both 1972), *The Sex Victims* and *Secrets of a Door to Door Salesman* (both 1973), *The Over Amorous Artist* (1974), *Feelings* (1975), *Intimate Games* (1976) and the short *The Kiss* (1977). She married a doctor and retired.

PRUDENCE DRAGE

A zany, red-headed comedienne in the Anna Quayle mould, Prudence Drage studied at RADA with Michael Armstrong, who cast her in his plays and later his films *Eskimo Nell* (1974), *Adventures of a Taxi Driver* (1975) and *Adventures of a Plumber's Mate* (1978). Her other films included *Virgin Witch* (1970), *A Clockwork Orange* (1971) and *The Sexplorer* (1975). She now works for a London solicitor.

Pete Walker

Fiona Richmond

Robin Askwith

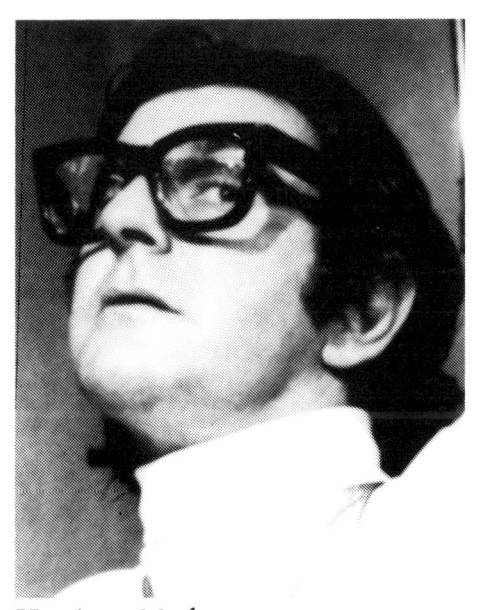

Harrison Marks

BARRY EVANS

Barry Evans' first leading screen role, as the gauche sixth-former Jamie McGregor, desperate to lose his virginity, in *Here We Go Round the Mulberry Bush* (1967), set him on the path to sex films. Despite a delightful performance as Jamie, it was then downhill all the way. He next appeared for Pete Walker in *Die Screaming Marianne* (1970), re-emerged in *Adventures of a Taxi Driver* (1975) for Stanley Long, and ended up in *Under the Doctor* (1976). His career picked up when he played "Sir" in the long-running (1977-81) TV comedy series *Mind Your Language* (also starring another sex film habitué, Françoise Pascal). He still acts and, in 1992, was involved in a strife-torn provincial tour of a whodunnit called *Anybody for Murder*.

ADRIENNE FANCEY

The eldest child of E.J. Fancey, Adrienne began as an actress, and appeared as Adrienne Scott in her father's production *Rock You Sinners* (1957). She gave up performing in favour of administration and, assisted by her brother Malcolm, took over her father's companies after his retirement in the Seventies. Adrienne continued distributing, and occasionally producing, low budget sex films, some in partnership with David Grant. The turning point came in 1974, when she bought, sight unseen, a French film called *Emmanuelle*. During more than two years at London's Prince Charles cinema, it took a million pounds at the box office, and encouraged Adrienne to expand upmarket. In the years that followed she distributed such films as Wes Craven's *The Hills Have Eyes* (1977), Barry Brown's *Cloud Dancer* (1979) and David Cronenberg's *Scanners* (1980) and produced a relatively big budget erotic drama, *The World Is Full of Married Men* (1979). But later films, notably *Butterfly* (1981), starring nine day wonder Pia Zadora, and *The Golden Seal* (1983), died at the box office, and Adrienne's last film as a producer, *The Hills Have Eyes Part II* (1985), was released straight to video in Britain. Adrienne is still in charge of her father's last surviving company, New Realm, but its halcyon days are but a memory. The staff has been reduced to just two - Adrienne and her stalwart assistant Paul Hennessey - and, having abandoned production and distribution, the company now acts as an agent for ancilliary film sales (renting other companies' product to hotels, airlines and shipping companies). Seemingly undaunted, Adrienne can still be seen, as glamorous and formidable as ever, at the Cannes Film Festival each spring.

E(dwin). J. FANCEY

Distributor and producer E.J. Fancey was, together with members of his two families, a major force in minor movies, and responsible for launching many successful careers. He was active in films from the Thirties, when he distributed Goldwyn and Selznick pictures in Britain. By the end of World War II, however, he had shifted gear into the production and distribution of poverty row comedies and melodramas, mostly released as second features; he was to remain number one in his field until the arrival of Michael Klinger and Tony Tenser at the turn of the Sixties. Fancey's companies - E.J. Fancey Ltd., New Realm, D.U.K. and S.F. - released *Down Among the Z Men* (1952) starring up-and-coming radio comedians Peter Sellers, Harry Secombe and Spike Milligan; *Rock You Sinners* (1957), the first British rock 'n' roll film, now believed lost; and all Michael Winner's early films including his nudie *Some Like It Cool* (1961). During the Sixties the Fancey companies produced and/or distributed hundreds of sex and horror pictures including at least one made by most of the directors in this book: Pete Walker, Arnold Louis Miller, Michael Armstrong, Malcolm Leigh, David Grant, Joe McGrath, Ray Selfe *et al.* Fancey's children by his wife, B.C. Fancey, are Adrienne and Malcolm Fancey, who took control of New Realm after their father's retirement. E.J. Fancey also had another two children, Judith Smith (a film editor) and Charles Negus-Fancey (not in the business), by his common law wife, Olive Negus, usually billed as Negus-Fancey, who ran Border Films and later Carlyle Pictures and Watchgrove. E.J. Fancey died on 28th October, 1980, at the age of 79.

MALCOLM FANCEY
Always in the shadow of his more dynamic sister Adrienne, Malcolm Fancey directed a documentary, *Crocodile Safari*, in 1967, and maintained a presence at New Realm throughout the Seventies, taking co-producer or associate producer credits on several sex films including *Secrets of a Door to Door Salesman* (1973), *The Over Amorous Artist* (1974), *I'm Not Feeling Myself Tonight!* (1975), *Girls Come First* (1975) and finally *The World Is Full of Married Men* (1979). He resigned from New Realm and left the film business in 1981. He now lives on the south coast of England with his wife, an American heiress.

SALLY FAULKNER
This RADA trained actress spent the whole of the Seventies playing leads in sex and horror films - and survived. Her filmography, which takes in both *Macbeth* and *Confessions of a Driving Instructor*, is, to say the least, odd. 1968: *Hot Millions*. 1969: *The Body Stealers*. 1971: *Macbeth*. 1972: *Layout for 5 Models*. 1974: *Vampyres*. 1975: *I'm Not Feeling Myself Tonight!* 1976: *Confessions of a Driving Instructor*. 1977: *Prey*. 1979: *Confessions from the David Galaxy Affair* a.k.a. *Star Sex*, *Jaguar Lives*. 1990: *The Fool*. She now appears

constantly on television; recently she has been in episodes of *Kinsey*, *Love Hurts* and *EastEnders*.

DEREK FORD
Compiling a complete filmography for Derek Ford is not easy as he has worked in various parts of the world and claims not to remember the names of all the films he directed. 1960: *Paris Playgirls* (co-director). 1961: *Los tres que robbaran una banco* (in Spain). 1969: *A Promise of Bed, Groupie Girl, The Wife Swappers*. 1971: *Suburban Wives, Secret Rites*. 1972: *Commuter Husbands*. 1973: *Keep It Up, Jack!* 1975: *The Sexplorer, Sex Express*. 1977: *What's Up Nurse*. 1978: *What's Up Superdoc*. 1982: *The House of Orchids* (in Italy). 1984: *Don't Open 'til Christmas* (co-director). 1985: *Blood Tracks* (in Sweden). 1990: *Urge to Kill. Sex Express* was released in the U.S. as *Diversions* with added hard core footage which Ford says he didn't direct. He is also credited as the director of the Italian film *Erotic Fantasies* (1978), but says that he directed none of it. Ford has recently branched out into a new career as a novelist. His two books to date, both with movie themes, are *Panic on Sunset* (1989) and *Casting Couch* (1990). The latter, written under the pseudonym "Selwyn Ford", was a joint effort with Alan Selwyn, a wheeler dealer for, and occasional performer in, many sex films of the Seventies. Ford is now working on his third book, *Bella*, about the tempestuous affaire between 20th Century-Fox executive Darryl F. Zanuck and actress Bella Darvi.

DAVID GRANT
The British sex film business produced no one approaching the notoriety of David Hamilton Grant, and if everything the tabloid press wrote about him is true, he is a monster who has "corrupted thousands of children." As Mr Grant is not around to defend himself, however, we must keep an open mind. Grant made two sex education films, *Love Variations* (1969) and *Love and Marriage* (1970), and for the remainder of the Seventies was a prolific producer of rubbish (mostly shorts and featurettes) for his Oppidan company. 1972: *Sinderella*. 1973: *Snow White and the Seven Perverts*. 1973: *Secrets of a Door to Door Salesman* (feature). 1974: *The Over Amorous Artist, The Great McGonagall* (feature). 1975: *Pink Orgasm* (unfinished), *Girls Come First*. 1976: *Under the Bed* (& directed), *The Office Party* (& directed), *Escape to Entebbe* (& directed). 1977: *The Kiss, Dear Margery Boobs, End of Term* (& directed), *Marcia* (& directed). 1978: *You're Driving Me Crazy!* (& directed). He then formed World of Video 2000 and in 1984 was jailed for eighteen months for distributing *Nightmares in a Damaged Brain* (1981), a well-made psycho thriller, with effects by Tom Savini, which was judged obscene during

the "video nasty" panic. From 1981 Grant spent much of his time in Cyprus, where he bought several properties including a villa, a delicatessen called Mr Piggy, and a club called the Pink Camel. In 1988, when he was deported from the island after he hit his girlfriend's husband over the head with a spade, *The Sun* alleged that he had been using his premises to make kiddie porn films with local children, and to trade in heroin and cocaine. Reporter Neil Syson admitted that the Cyprus police had no proof of these allegations. Grant moved on to Ankara, Turkey, but in October, 1988, he was back in England, where he told magistrates at Staines, Middlesex, that he could not afford to pay a £150 fine for drunken driving. David Grant has not been seen in this country since then. In 1989 he and a man named Amin Rajabali were charged with video copyright offences, but Grant failed to appear in court. The Turkish newspaper *Milliyet* reported that he was now living in a house in Side, on the southern Turkish coast, belonging to a government official. But in 1990, at the video copyright trial at which Rajabali was found guilty, Grant was said to be "languishing in a Turkish jail." There have been no further reports of Grant's whereabouts, but in 1992 three people interviewed by the author were of the opinion that he was dead, possibly by murder.

MICHAEL GREEN

Veteran producer and distributor Michael Green has been in the business since 1934. In the Seventies he ran Variety, a lowly distributor, and produced sex films, e.g. *Keep It Up, Jack!* (1973), *It Could Happen to You* (1975), *What's Up Nurse* (1977) and *What's Up Superdoc* (1978). He then formed Entertainment Distributors and subsequently Entertainment in Video, which have developed into quite a force in the market-place despite the purchase of some resounding duds (*Split Second, Until the End of the World*).

PAMELA GREEN

Pamela Green first appeared on screen in 1958 in Harrison Marks' glamour films *The Window Dresser, Xcitement, Gypsy Fire* and *Witches' Brew*. She was credited in the latter as "Rita Landré", a pseudonym she often used. In 1959 she was one of Carl Boehm's victims in *Peeping Tom*. She then starred in Marks' *Naked As Nature Intended* (1961), had one line in *The Day the Earth Caught Fire* (1962) and a cameo in *The Naked World of Harrison Marks* (1965). Ten years later she returned to the screen in *Legend of the Werewolf* (1975). The following year her photograph appeared in a TV movie, *The Prison* ("Director David Wickes needed a photo of a fat tart"). She's not the Pamela Green listed in the cast of *Under the Bed* (1976). After breaking up with Harrison Marks, Pamela began her present relationship with Douglas Webb,

Norman J. Warren

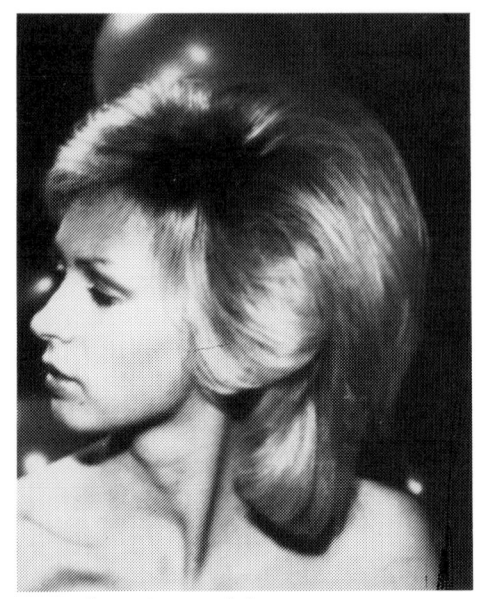

Monika Ringwald

Barry Evans

Sue Longhurst

the stills cameraman on *Naked As Nature Intended*. She describes herself as his "runner". In 1985 Douglas suffered a stroke and gave up film work. He and Pamela moved to the Isle of Wight in 1986 and began planning a coffee table book featuring a selection of Douglas' photographs of Pamela from 1961-1979. To finance the enterprise, Douglas sold the Distinguished Flying Medal he was awarded for his part in the 1943 Dam Busters raid; but the book remains unpublished. Douglas and Pamela now run a small studio specialising in weddings and portraiture. Pamela is a member of the Yarmouth Women's Institute and has sung in concerts all over the Isle of Wight. The couple, who have been together for well over 25 years, are considering marriage.

JOHN HAMILL

After studying drama at the Webber-Douglas Academy, John Hamill appeared in repertory at Westcliff-on-sea. For several years he played Dave Cartwright in TV's *Crossroads* and then went into the long-running stage comedy *There's a Girl in My Soup*. His film career began in 1968 with *A Dandy in Aspic*, and more supporting roles followed in *Every Home Should Have One, Trog, The Beast in the Cellar, No Blade of Grass, Tower of Evil, Travels with My Aunt* and *The National Health*. He then found a niche playing leads in sex comedies: *The Over Amorous Artist* (1974), *Girls Come First* (1975), *Under the Bed* (1976) and *Hardcore* (1977). In 1975 he began producing and directing himself in the sex comedy *Doing the Best I Can*, but this was left unfinished when Hamill's money ran out. Unable to find acting work, he opened a pine furnishers in south London. A comeback attempt in the Swedish film *Black Sun* (1979) was not a success. "The sex movies ruined my career," he said in 1983. "If I had the time over again, I'd do it differently. But you know how it is: I was out of work, the birds were smashing, and I've always been a born flasher."

ROBERT HARTFORD-DAVIS

After breaking into the business as an electrician at Teddington Studios, Hartford-Davis went to the U.S. to study at the University of California, then returned to Britain and worked as an assistant director. The exploitation films he directed in Britain from 1961-71 range from dreadful to dazzling, but most have their admirers, and it is only a matter of time before Hartford-Davis receives the acclaim denied him during his life. 1961: *Crosstrap*. 1963: *The Yellow Teddybears, Saturday Night Out*. 1964: *The Black Torment*. 1965: *Gonks Go Beat, The Sandwich Man*. 1967: *Corruption*. 1969: *The Smashing Bird I Used to Know*. 1970: *Incense for the Damned*. 1971: *The Fiend, Nobody Ordered Love*. Hartford-Davis then went to the U.S., where he directed two routine action pictures, *Black Gunn* (1972) and *The Take* (1974). He spent his remaining years in television and was working on a TV movie, *Murder in Peyton Place*, when he suffered a heart attack and died on 12th June, 1977, aged 54. The movie was completed by Bruce Kessler.

PENNY IRVING
This tiny, cute, giggly blonde proved surprisingly versatile, playing a dramatic lead in *House of Whipcord* (1974) and comic support in the TV series (1974-78) and film (1977) *Are You Being Served?* The rest of her film appearances were bits: *Big Zapper* (1973), *Carry On Dick*, *Percy's Progress* and *Vampira* (all 1974), *The Bawdy Adventures of Tom Jones* and *The Comeback* (both 1977). She was also a hostess for the TV game show *Mr and Mrs*.

PETER JESSOP
Most cameramen on sex films had little ability, often rendering the films cheap and ugly. Peter Jessop was a notable exception, who worked his way up from dogsbody at a Bournemouth documentary company to a highly efficient cameraman with a gift for atmospheric interior lighting. He was always in demand - and still is. After his documentary work, Jessop was a focus puller, first at Merton Park Studios on many B-features, then on two films for Joseph Losey. His first features as lighting cameraman were for Bachoo Sen - *Her Private Hell* (1967), *Loving Feeling* (1968) and the unfinished *To Rio For Love* (1970); he was Pete Walker's favourite cameraman, lighting ten of his films between 1970-78; and his other sex films include *Under the Bed* (1976), *The Office Party* (1976) and *You're Driving Me Crazy!* (1978) for David Grant, *Sex with the Stars* (1980) and *Nutcracker* (1982) for Anwar Kawadri, and *The Lifetaker* (1975), now remembered only because one of its nude scenes featured Peter Duncan, another actor who was to become a household name as a *Blue Peter* presenter. Since 1983, when he lit former sex film director Martin Campbell's mini-series *Charlie*, Jessop has worked mainly on television, often for award-winning producer Brian Eastman. His latest series are *G.B.H.*, *Jeeves and Wooster* and *Head Over Heels*. Jessop's camera operator on the Pete Walker films was Peter Sinclair (also Stanley Long's regular cameraman). Today, like Jessop, Sinclair works mainly for TV and in 1992 photographed the TV movie *Anna Lee*, directed by Colin Bucksey. This marked a notable reunion. On Pete Walker's *House of Mortal Sin*, Sinclair was the camera operator and Bucksey was the focus puller.

MARK JONES
Another of the handful of leading men in British sex films, Mark Jones was the

man next door type, sometimes bewigged, but usually bald. He was in *Layout for 5 Models* (1972), *Keep It Up, Jack!* (1973), *The Sexplorer* and *Secrets of a Superstud* (both 1975), *Marcia* (1977), *Can I Come Too?* (1979) and *Don't Open 'til Christmas* (1984). Nowadays he spends much of his time in Spain "having a good time and playing my guitar", but he returned to Britain to appear in the BBC series *Buccaneer* and to play the gentleman whose wig comes off in the Hamlet cigars commercial. He tells me he's writing a novel about life in the Sixties.

MICHAEL KEATERING

Michael Keatering was the pseudonym of Edward Craven Walker, an industrialist, who, in 1960, invented the "Astrolamp", a classic piece of Sixties kitsch (it's a table-lamp incorporating a transparent container of oily liquid, which forms ever-changing shapes when heated by the light bulb). Although one might assume that no-one with an iota of taste would give it house room, over seven million of the lamps have been sold throughout the world, and Walker still manufactures them from his factory in Bournemouth. A life-long sun-lover, Walker wanted to promote the naturist movement and, despite having no film-making experience, he produced and directed three films - *Travelling Light* (1959), *Sunswept* (1961) and *Eves on Skis* (1963). Walker regards these as Britain's only genuine naturist films and everything else as exploitative junk. In 1963 the nudie market was exhausted, and Walker never picked up a camera again. In the Seventies he founded the Bournemouth and District Outdoor Club, a naturist paradise which now has three hundred families as members. He is working on *Through Europe Naturally*, a guide to Europe for naturists.

JAMES KENELM CLARKE

It is to be hoped that, before too much longer, James Kenelm Clarke will realise the error of his ways and return to making the TV documentaries for which he has undoubted ability. His future as a feature film director does not look bright. A writer-researcher at Anglia television from 1960, he joined the BBC in 1967 and directed documentaries there, mainly for the *Man Alive* series, until 1976. His first feature film, shot as *Colorado Stone* in 1973, was finally released in 1978 as *Sweet Virgin*. Of the three sex films he made starring Fiona Richmond, only the first, *Exposé* (1975), has any merit. (It has been banned in Britain since 1984). After a long lay-off, Kenelm Clarke returned to film-making with *Funny Money* (1982), one of the unfunniest comedies ever made, and the similarly humourless *Yellow Pages* (1983), shelved for five years before popping up as *Going Undercover*. He has since tried to set up projects

- including a re-make of *Exposé* - in the U.S., but so far without success.

MICHAEL KLINGER

Producer Michael Klinger evidently saw himself as a movie mogul in the classic Hollywood tradition, a role for which he was physically well suited. But he was never able to break free from the shackles of sexploitation, which was his true metier. Born in Soho, the son of an immigrant Polish tailor, Klinger was a disc jockey before managing Soho's Nell Gwynn strip club. One day Tony Tenser, then head of publicity for Miracle Films, called on Klinger to hire his strippers for a Miracle publicity stunt. The men became partners and, in 1960, opened three cinemas including the Compton, London's first cinema club. The men's next venture, Compton-Cameo Films, produced and distributed sex films including Harrison Marks' *Naked As Nature Intended* (1961) and most of the Arnold Louis Miller/Stanley Long productions. By 1964 the company was doing sufficiently well to invest £97,000 in Roman Polanski's first British film, *Repulsion*. But this, and Polanski's next film, *Cul de Sac* (1966), were among Compton-Cameo's rare bids for critical approval. Klinger and Tenser split in 1967. Klinger launched his own company with two highly sensational properties, *The Penthouse* (1967), in which a woman is terrorised and raped in a penthouse flat by two intruders, and *Baby Love* (1968), based on the Tina Chad Christian best-seller about an orphaned nymphet who seduces the three members of her adoptive family. *Baby Love* introduced Klinger's protégée Linda Hayden, who was to appear, to her decreasing advantage, in other Klinger productions. Klinger hit his peak in the early Seventies with two exciting thrillers, *Get Carter* (1971) and *Pulp* (1972), both starring Michael Caine. He then produced a couple of action adventures, *Gold* (1974) and *Shout at the Devil* (1976), in South Africa, and slipped back into his old ways with the *Confessions* series (1974-77). Klinger's subsequent films had little appeal, and his last, *Riding High* (1980), based on a story by Derek Ford, was a disaster that very nearly ruined him. He died of a heart attack at the age of 68 on 15th September, 1989.

MALCOLM LEIGH

Malcolm Leigh is a somewhat mysterious individual, with a taste for the exotic and the occult, who appears to have both sprung from and returned to documentary film-making. His first films, all for Negus-Fancey, were *The Window Cleaner* (1968), a short sex film; *Legend of the Witches* (1969), a documentary about present-day witchcraft; *Well of Time* (1970), a travelogue about Thailand; and *Games That Lovers Play* (1970), his only narrative feature. After two more shorts, *Erotic Fantasies* (1971) and *The Sword and the Geisha*

(1971), a documentary about Japanese traditions, Leigh seemed to disappear. In fact he continued to make films, and three more have been traced: *Pillars of Islam* (1973) is about Arab customs during Ramadan; *Manifestations of Shiva* (1980), shown on British television in 1986, shows the worship of the Hindu god of life; and *Sleepsong* (1985) is a short fantasy. This is a remarkable body of work distinguished by real flair for colour, composition and sound design.

MORTON LEWIS

A noted Wardour Street veteran, Morton Lewis has been in the film business since 1931 and a fourth division director since 1952. He directed only one sex film, *Secrets of a Superstud* (1975), but produced several others including Derek Ford's *Commuter Husbands* (1972) and *The Sexplorer* (1975). Lewis' abiding interest is soccer. He produced (and Donald and Derek Ford wrote) *The World at Their Feet* (1970), the official record of the 1970 World Cup in Mexico, and now owns the world's biggest library of World Cup footage, which he supervises from his home in south London. Last year he wrote *Ted "Kid" Lewis: His Life and Times*, a biography of his father, the boxer.

JOHN LINDSAY

While working as a stills photographer for Stanley Long in the late Sixties, John Lindsay was inspired to begin making blue movies. Throughout the Seventies, he was Britain's leading practitioner, with the highest profile. As early as 1971 Long filmed Lindsay at work for his documentary *Naughty!* and recorded his comments about pornography ("I would like to stress that the girls I use in my films are nice girls. Because they screw and have it up here and up there and in their mouths and that, this doesn't mean to say that they're not nice girls"). The standard of Lindsay's productions is contested. In 1975, after he was found not guilty of obscenity at Birmingham Crown Court, Lindsay opened Britain's first hard core cinema clubs and, for the next eight years, resisted every official attempt to shut them down. But in 1983 he received a tip-off from a friendly detective at New Scotland Yard that orders had been received from the highest authority to put Lindsay out of business by any means necessary. Lindsay fled to Holland, but missed his twin daughters, returned to England and was arrested. At his trial in London, Lindsay was convicted of obscenity on the strength of four videotapes which thirteen policemen swore had been found at one of Lindsay's clubs. Lindsay claims that the tapes, which featured homosexual rape and other graphic violence that would have been of no interest to his clientèle, were planted. "I would have convicted me on those tapes," he said. "They were disgusting." He was sentenced to twelve months imprisonment. Lindsay sold his clubs to a Maltese organisation, but it was swiftly harassed out of England by the new licensing regulations. Upon his release, Lindsay was approached by the Inland Revenue, which claimed that it was owed £3.5 million in back taxes, but was willing to settle for £100,000. Lindsay refused to pay a penny. A seafarer for many years (he bought his first yacht in 1978), Lindsay moved to Kent, where he now runs a marine broking company. "Don't give anyone my telephone number," he begged me. "I lead a peaceful life down here."

STANLEY LONG

Although he has been in the business for well over thirty years, Stanley Long was a feature film director for only seven of them. 1964: *Circlorama Cavalcade* (co-director). 1971: *Bread, Naughty!* 1972: *Sex and the Other Woman*. 1973: *On the Game*. 1975: *It Could Happen to You* a.k.a. *Intimate Teenage Secrets, Adventures of a Taxi Driver*. 1977: *Adventures of a Private Eye*. 1978: *Adventures of a Plumber's Mate*. Between 1982-83 he used the pseudonym Al Beresford to direct three shorts - *Dream House, That's the Way to Do It* and *Do You Believe in Fairies?* - which were later linked and issued on video as *Scream Time*. Although he could easily retire - in 1982 he sold his distributor Alpha to Intervision for £1.8 million - Long still works five days a week in Soho, running an aviation company and the largest film equipment rental service in Europe. He has held a commercial pilot's licence for many years and flies all over Europe in his Cessna Golden Eagle. Does he miss the creative side of the business? "No," he states categorically. "I don't have to get up at 6 a.m. any more."

SUE LONGHURST

The English rose of sex films, Sue Longhurst was considerably older than her contemporaries, making her screen debut in a Swedish film, *Champagnegalopp*, in 1959. Although it is hard to believe, she was pushing thirty when she appeared as a schoolgirl in her first British film, *Lust for a Vampire* (1970). Her later films included *Secrets of a Door to Door Salesman* and *Keep It Up Jack!* (both 1973), *Can You Keep It Up for a Week?*, *The Over Amorous Artist* and *What the Swedish Butler Saw* (all 1974), *Girls Come First* (1975), *Keep It Up Downstairs* (1976), *Come Play with Me* (1977) and *Can I Come Too?* (1979). In poor health in recent years, she is now completely retired.

SUZY MANDEL

One of the more accomplished sex film starlets, Suzy Mandel played the lead in *Intimate Games* (1976) and was also a regular on Benny Hill's TV shows. Her other films were *Confessions of a Driving Instructor* (1976), *Come Play with Me* (1977), *Adventures of a Plumber's Mate*, *The Playbirds* and *You're Driving Me Crazy!* (all 1978). She then married property tycoon Stanley Margolis and moved with him to the U.S., where she continued to act, sometimes in hard core. She starred in *Blonde Ambition* (1980), seen in Britain, heavily cut, in 1984.

HARRISON MARKS
George Harrison Marks shot his first glamour film in 1958 and is still in production (on video) today - an unsurpassed record in the British sex film industry. His oeuvre encompasses only five feature films - *Naked As Nature Intended* (1961), *The Naked World of Harrison Marks* (1965), *Pattern of Evil* (1967), *The Nine Ages of Nakedness* (1969) and *Come Play with Me* (1977) - but more than five hundred motion pictures in all. His current preoccupation is with corporal punishment. He publishes and edits *Kane* magazine and in 1984 began producing and directing spanking videotapes, a possibly unique throwback to the moral values (and production standards) of another age. In *Five of the Best* (1988) a group of randy businessmen metes out corrective training to squealing dolly birds. One gentleman is chastising a bare-bottomed bimbo across his knee when his false moustache begins to peel away from his upper lip. He presses it back into position, glances to the camera for instruction, and appears to be told to carry on - which he does. In 1991 Marks returned to his roots by producing an evening of variety at London's Shaw Theatre. Top of the bill was comedienne Joan Turner, who played Marilyn Chambers' auntie in *Insatiable* (1980). The event was sparsely attended, but Marks is determined "to bring back the spirit of variety into the theatres" and plans further shows.

STEPHANIE MARRIAN
A pencil-slim model with long, auburn hair and a refined demeanour, Stephanie Marrian played a handful of supporting roles in *The Hot Girls*, *Can You Keep It Up For a Week?* and *Confessions of a Sex Maniac* (all 1974) and *The Sexplorer* (1975). She inched into mainstream movies - *The World Is Full of Married Men* (1979) and Mel Brooks' *History of the World Part I* (1981) - then appeared to stop work.

DAVID McGILLIVRAY
Having knocked around the film industry since 1964, I began writing screen-

Stanley Long

John Hamill

plays for exploitation movies in 1973. Among those filmed were four for Pete Walker (*House of Whipcord, Frightmare, House of Mortal Sin, Schizo*), two for Norman J. Warren (*Satan's Slave, Terror*) and one for Joe McGrath (*I'm Not Feeling Myself Tonight!*). I've also worked in various capacities for Ray Selfe, John Lindsay, Adrienne and Malcolm Fancey, Stanley Long, Michael Armstrong, James Kenelm Clarke and Dick Randall. My last film, written for Ray Selfe in 1983, was released direct to video as *Turnaround* in 1988. Also in 1983 the magazine articles which formed the basis of this book inspired a film made for the BBC television series *Omnibus*. In it I interviewed Harrison Marks, Pamela Green, Nat Miller, John Trevelyan and Iseult Richardson, daughter of Spielplatz founder Charles Macaskie. The film was considered unsuitable for broadcast and is now untraceable. In recent years I have written and directed several plays all over Britain and in Cape Town and Los Angeles. Sex does not feature in them.

JOE McGRATH

If anyone could have extracted real humour from the British sex comedy, it ought to have been award-winning comedy director Joe McGrath, famous for his work with Peter Cook and Dudley Moore on the classic TV series *Not Only...But Also*. In fact McGrath's sex comedies rank with the very worst, which suggests that the genre was so unworkable that it would have defeated even Preston Sturges. Formerly a theatre and TV set designer, McGrath turned director via *Candid Camera* and was henceforth typed as a comedy man. He directed two silly but very amusing films, *Thirty Is a Dangerous Age, Cynthia* (1967) and *The Bliss of Mrs Blossom* (1968), but they were not wildly successful, and by 1973 he was sufficiently under-employed to accept work from the Fanceys and David Grant. With a pseudonymous Denis Norden he wrote *Secrets of a Door to Door Salesman* (1973), then directed *The Great McGonagall* (1974), *I'm Not Feeling Myself Tonight!* (1975), *Girls Come First* (1975) and the short *Escape to Entebbe* (1976). He was tempted away from TV commercials to direct Morecambe and Wise's agonising swan song *Night Train to Murder* (1985). In 1992 it was announced that he was in Russia directing George Segal in something called *Festival*.

ARNOLD LOUIS MILLER

When the articles which formed the basis of this book were first published in the magazine *Cinema*, Arnold Louis Miller took exception to my allegation that his unbearable travelogues were "regularly booed off the screen in Hampstead and Kensington, but apparently accepted without murmur everywhere else." Marvel Comics, the publishers of *Cinema*, received a letter from

Miller's solicitors announcing his intention to sue. If the case had ever come to court, the defence would have called any number of Hampstead and Kensington residents, who would have sworn on oath that the title "Global-Queensway presents" was regularly greeted with groans of despair. But no action was taken. In a letter, Marvel's solicitor pointed out that my implication was that Global-Queensway travelogues were enjoyed by the majority of the population, and that this could hardly be considered libellous. I never heard from Miller again. It seems that his last short was *Double Decker Fun* (1983), made for the National Children's Home. Rumour has it that he now teaches at a London film school.

NAT MILLER

Nat Miller was one of the most fondly-regarded old boys of Wardour Street. He alone took the trouble to write and thank me for what I'd written about him in my original articles about British sex films. In 1983 I insisted that he be included in the BBC television film based on the articles. He invited us into his office for the interview and I remember that he skirted around the subject of *Nudist Paradise*, preferring to be remembered as the distributor of the Japanese art house picture *Onibaba*. I had no idea that he was already ill with leukaemia. He died just before Christmas that year at the age of 74. His death warranted one paragraph in a trade paper.

MARY MILLINGTON

Mary Millington appeared in *Keep It Up Downstairs* and *Intimate Games* (both 1976), *Come Play with Me* (1977), *What's Up Superdoc* and *The Playbirds* (both 1978), *Confessions from the David Galaxy Affair* a.k.a. *Star Sex*, *The Great Rock 'n' Roll Swindle* and *Queen of the Blues* (all 1979). The last two years of her life appear to have been intolerable. She was hooked on cocaine and receiving psychiatric treatment for depression. In 1977 she was prosecuted for possession of obscene magazines, but acquitted. "I am a very moral person," she told reporters after the trial. In 1978 she was again in trouble with the police, this time on a shoplifting charge later dropped. Tax inspectors were pressing her for a million pounds and her husband had told her that he wanted a divorce. In 1979 Mary was once again arrested for shoplifting. She was found dead at her home in Banstead, Surrey, on 19th August, 1979, having taken an overdose of pills washed down with vodka. She was 34. "The police have made my life a misery," she wrote in a suicide note.

MARGARET NOLAN

She was no great shakes as an actress, but comedy producers took a liking to Margaret Nolan, and no other glamour girl of the Sixties had a longer or more successful screen career. Anyone who watched British television during the late Sixties and early Seventies was familiar with her half-closed eyes and Bardot pout. Under the name Vicky Kennedy, she appeared in glamour films for Stanley Long and Harrison Marks. Chosen by Maurice Binder to be the girl in gold paint behind the main titles of *Goldfinger* (1964), she went on to play "blonde" or "girl" in several other films. But she also had substantial comedy roles as the art mistress in *The Great St Trinian's Train Robbery* (1965) and a prostitute in *No Sex Please - We're British* (1973), and was a *Carry On* regular from 1965 to 1974. Her last acting work was done in the late Seventies.

FRANÇOISE PASCAL

Actress Françoise Pascal very nearly made the grade, but wild living took its toll, and most people remember her today only as Richard Johnson's girlfriend. Born on Mauritius of Anglo-French parentage, she came to London to work as a model. In 1968 she was in two sex films, Norman J. Warren's *Loving Feeling* and Pete Walker's *School For Sex*, as well as Jean-Luc Godard's *Sympathy For the Devil*. Later there were better roles in *There's a Girl in My Soup* (1970), *Burke and Hare* (1971) and *Soft Beds, Hard Battles* (1973), but her next, and final, film was *Keep It Up Downstairs* (1976). Until the early Eighties, she was popular on television, both as the girl in the Manikin cigar commercials and the French student in the comedy series *Mind Your Language*. But her "private" life was already making the headlines. For most of the Seventies she lived with Richard Johnson, by whom she had a son, Nicholas. Her first set of kiss-and-tell revelations concerned her tortuous relationship with the ageing playboy actor and her subsequent affair with racing driver Adrian Reynard. In 1982 she went to the U.S., where she played bits in episodes of *The Love Boat* and *Hart to Hart*, but mainly hung around with Hollywood's jet set. In 1986 she told the *News of the World* that she had been working as a cocaine pusher to what sounded like most of Hollywood's British acting fraternity, and that she had bedded an almost farcical list of international celebrities including Warren Beatty, Sacha Distel, tennis player Ilie Nastase and a singer with the vocal group Manhattan Transfer. In 1989 she was back in London, claiming that she wanted to reactivate her acting career.

HILARY PRITCHARD

A talented comic actress who first made an impression in the Sixties TV series *Braden's Week*, Hilary Pritchard was soon ensconced in sex films: *What's*

Good For the Goose (1969), *She'll Follow You Anywhere* (1971), *The Over Amorous Artist* and *All I Want Is You...and You...and You* (both 1974), *Under the Doctor* (1976) and *Adventures of a Private Eye* (1977). In 1973 she was also in the London stage version of *No Sex Please - We're British*.

FIONA RICHMOND

In sharp contrast to the real-life excesses of such doomed sex goddesses as Mary Millington and Françoise Pascal, Fiona Richmond's debauchery was all an act. She retained complete control over her life and now claims to have found contentment as a wife and mother. Fiona was a Playboy bunny when she auditioned successfully for the part of a swimmer in Paul Raymond's stage comedy *Pyjama Tops* (1971). She then became a writer for Raymond's magazine *Men Only* and caused much ballyhoo travelling the world, "road-testing" men. She admitted later that her reports were pure fiction. She appeared in more Raymond stage productions - *Let's Get Laid!* (1974), *Come Into My Bed* (1976), and *Women Behind Bars* (1977) - and wrote her autobiography, *Fiona* (1976), and other books. Her films were *Barry McKenzie Holds His Own* (1974), *Exposé* (1975), *Hardcore* and *Let's Get Laid!* (both 1977), *History of the World Part I* (1981) and *Eat the Rich* (1987). Britain's number one sex symbol until the arrival of the raunchier Mary Millington, Fiona nursed an unfulfilled ambition. "What I'd really like to do," she revealed, "is develop into Britain's answer to Lucille Ball." In 1983 she married TV presenter James Montgomery and had her first child at the age of forty. She still guests occasionally on radio and television; in 1992 she took part in the TV programme *Myths of Motherhood*.

MONIKA RINGWALD

One of the loveliest sex film starlets, German-born Monika Ringwald played the title role in *The Sexplorer* (1975) plus several other bits: *Confessions of a Window Cleaner* and *Confessions of a Sex Maniac* (both 1974), *I'm Not Feeling Myself Tonight!* and *Erotic Inferno* (both 1975), *Intimate Games* and *Satan's Slave* (both 1976) and *What's Up Nurse* (1977). In 1978 she married a car dealer and retired.

PETER ROGERS

Although all 31 *Carry On* films have been directed by the same man, Gerald Thomas, even he has confessed that he is little more than a ringmaster putting the cast through their hoops. The man who invented the *Carry On* concept, thought up the idea for each episode, and thereby re-popularised off-colour, music-hall humour and promulgated it throughout the world as something pleasurably British is the series' producer, Peter Rogers, a man of vastly underrated influence. A music-hall lover (needless to say), he was a reporter and a radio scriptwriter before joining Rank to write religious shorts. After World War II he worked with, and later married, Betty Box, clearly a woman after his own heart: she went on to produce the *Doctor* series (1953-1970)* and the two *Percy* films (1970 and 1974). Rogers was not only responsible for the *Carry On* series (1958-1992), the longest in film history, but also several other successful comedies with cheeky titles including *Please Turn Over* (1960), *Raising the Wind* (1961) and *The Big Job* (1965). *Carry On Behind* (1975), *Carry On England* (1976) and *Carry On Emmannuelle* (1978), all made without the much-loved Sidney James and writer Talbot Rothwell, and released in competition with the dirtier *Confessions* and *Adventures* films, were failures, and throughout the Eighties Rogers was unable to find the backing for further episodes. Instead he produced compilations of *Carry On* extracts for television. Against almighty odds - after 14 years does a *Carry On* audience still exist? - *Carry On Columbus* went into production in 1992. Rogers, now in his late seventies, was promoted to executive producer.

RAY SELFE
Virtually unknown outside the skid row film community, Ray Selfe is a household name within it as an exhibitor, producer, director, cameraman, editor, performer and all-round film fan. On the periphery of the business since 1948, he was a sex film recruit in 1970, when he produced and (as Howard Edward) photographed *Sweet and Sexy*. He was then an adviser for the 3-D sequences in Pete Walker's *The Four Dimensions of Greta* (1972), the director of *White Cargo* (1973), and a cameraman on *The Hot Girls* (1974). In 1972 Selfe opened the Pigalle cinema in a former strip club on Piccadilly Circus. In need of extra finance, Selfe went into partnership with producer David Grant and became a director of Grant's Oppidan company, which

---

* Although their *raison d'être* was their bedpan humour, the seven *Doctor* films, inspired by the novels of Richard Gordon, seem once removed from low comedy and closer in spirit to Ealing traditions. The films were civilised, well-mounted and used actors rather than comedians. Perhaps it was because they had class and a literary source that they were treated far more indulgently by the censor than the lewder *Carry On* series. Two very suggestive jokes in *Doctor* films of the Fifties caused such astonishment that they have passed into the annals of great British humour. Most people are still familiar with James Robertson Justice's demand "You! What's the bleeding time?", and the exchange while Dirk Bogarde is examining a nubile, female patient ("Big breaths!", "Yeth, and I'm only thixteen").

eventually operated eight sex cinemas (seven straight, one gay), and produced and distributed exploitation films. Selfe produced Grant's *Under the Bed* (1976) and appeared in *You're Driving Me Crazy!* (1978). A highly profitable operation ("We were just in the right place at the right time," says Selfe) came to an end in 1978 when the Pigalle site, with Oppidan's offices above it, was earmarked for redevelopment. Selfe directed one more film, *Can I Come Too?* (1979), directed the prologue of *Emmanuelle in Soho* (1981), and then worked on three horror films for American producer Dick Randall. Since 1987 he has plundered his huge collection of public domain material to produce compilations for video release. Recent titles include *The Young Duke* and *Charlie - A Celebration* (both 1989), *Hollywood Song and Dance* (1990), *Goddess in the Raw* and *Movie Nostalgia* (both 1991).

BACHOO SEN

Sen, in Britain from 1952, joined forces in the Sixties with Richard Schulman to produce and distribute sex pictures. The partnership broke up in 1972. Schulman, who plays a silent role as an Arabian judge in the opening sequence of Antony Balch's *Secrets of Sex* (1969), went on to manage the Shaftesbury Theatre. Sen stayed in the sex film business, setting up the English Film Company. Unlike Balch, Sen never mastered the art of re-titling, and his foreign porn played British cinemas under such cumbersome billings as *Sexier Than Sex* and *The Sex of Their Bodies*. After producing *Erotic Inferno* (1975), Sen fell ill and it seemed unlikely that he would work again. But in 1986 he re-emerged in Florida as the producer of the inane and trashy *Nightmare Weekend*.

LINDSAY SHONTEFF

Canadian-born Lindsay Shonteff is still at work in Britain and - oblivious to trends, economics and public taste - still committed to his favourite genre, the espionage adventure. 1963: *Devil Doll*. 1964: *Curse of Simba*. 1966: *Run with the Wind*. 1967: *Sumuru*. 1969: *Clegg*. 1969: *Night After Night After Night*. 1970: *Permissive*. 1971: *The Yes Girls*. 1972: *The Fast Kill*. 1973: *Big Zapper*. 1974: *The Sworsdsman*. 1975: *Spy Story*. 1977: *No. 1 of the Secret Service*. 1979: *Licensed to Love and Kill*. 1980: *The Man from SEX, Combat Zone*. 1985: *How Sleep the Brave*. 1986: *Lipstick and Blood* (video), *The Killing Edge* (video). 1990: *Number One Gun*. Shonteff's next project is called *Gunfighter*.

MURRAY SMITH

Murray Smith helped put director Pete Walker on the map with his screenplays for *Cool It Carol!* and *Die Screaming, Marianne* (both 1970), *The Four Dimensions of Greta* (1972) and, to a lesser extent, *The Comeback* (1977) and *Home Before Midnight* (1978). He also wrote *The Sellout* (1976) and *Bear Island* (1980). In recent years he has worked exclusively for television, scripting episodes of *The XYY Man, Strangers, Dempsey and Makepeace, Bulman, The Paradise Club* and many other series. He formed a company with author Frederick Forsyth to produce six TV movies screened from 1989-90. Smith's first novel, *Corrida*, is published in 1993.

BOBBY SPARROW

Blonde ex-dancer in brief sex film roles: *The Over Amorous Artist* and *Confessions of a Sex Maniac* (1974), *Girls Come First, Confessions of a Pop Performer, I'm Not Feeling Myself Tonight!* and *Secrets of a Superstud* (all 1975), *To the Devil a Daughter* (1976).

DAVID SULLIVAN

There can be very few people who are unaware of what became of former film tycoon David Sullivan but, for the record, Sullivan first published the *Sunday Sport* in September, 1986. The Wednesday edition appeared in 1988, the Friday edition in 1989, and the newspaper has been daily since August, 1991. Companies connected with the Sullivan empire also own half Britain's licenced sex shops. The latest estimate of Sullivan's personal fortune is £65 million (more than that of Michael Caine and Rod Stewart put together).

TONY TENSER

The British film industry is gasping its last because there is no one like Tony Tenser to kick it back to life. In the late Sixties, when colour television was the Big Thing and half a dozen American studios pulled out of British production with no intention of returning, the industry was at crisis point; and yet there was Tony Tenser, still finding the finance for new projects, discovering new, inexperienced directors, and getting the films made, good and bad. He was the Irving Thalberg of the exploitation movie and, like the boy wonder of M-G-M, his career was too short. Even back in the days of Compton-Cameo, Tenser knew which side his bread was buttered. It was his partner, Michael Klinger, who wanted to take a risk with Roman Polanski and a script about a young woman going out of her mind. Tenser preferred the somewhat safer bet of Harrison Marks and a lot of young women taking their clothes off. When the pair sold Compton-Cameo in 1967, Tenser formed Tony Tenser Films, which rapidly became Tigon. One of his first releases was a five year old ghost story, *Carnival of Souls*, which was to be restored and revered as a cult in 1990. Tigon British Productions gave opportunities to such tyro directors as Michael Reeves, Menachem Golan, Michael Armstrong, John Bown, Stephen Weeks, Piers Haggard and even Graham Stark. Tenser says that he resigned from Tigon in 1972 because he disliked making films with graphic violence. He moved to Southport, Lancs., where he imported wicker furniture for two years and then started a business acquiring and leasing property. He has recently begun appearing at movie conventions to talk about his illustrious career.

JOHN TREVELYAN

If John Trevelyan had not come along when he did, perhaps British screen actors might still be required to kiss each other with their mouths closed. An examiner at the B.B.F.C. from 1951, Trevelyan prided himself on his liberal attitudes, and no sooner had he become Secretary of the Board in 1958 than he passed *Room at the Top*, franker about sex than any previous British film. The scene in which Heather Sears submitted to Laurence Harvey's advances on a river bank ("Be gentle with me") caused many young men to get very hot under the collar indeed. Trevelyan was similarly lenient with many other films of artistic merit, and it is curious to reflect that, until the early Sixties, British audiences regularly saw material that was cut by censorship boards in the U.S. But Trevelyan, in common with most other censors, had double standards and, during his regime, sex films were sometimes butchered to incomprehensibility. One of his last acts, before retiring in the summer of 1971, was to reduce Russ Meyer's 1968 film *Vixen* from 71 to 47 minutes. The first British censor with a high public profile, Trevelyan continued to appear on the media and serve on committees (including that of Exit, the voluntary euthanasia organisation) until his death on 15th August, 1986, at the age of 83.

PETE WALKER

The Boss, as far as British exploitation films are concerned, Pete Walker has been in retirement since 1983. His films are *I Like Birds* (1967), *Strip Poker* and *School For Sex* (both 1968), *Man of Violence, Cool It Carol!* and *Die Screaming, Marianne* (all 1970), *The Four Dimensions of Greta* and *The Flesh and Blood Show* (both 1972), *Tiffany Jones* (1973), *House of Whipcord* and *Frightmare* (both 1974), *House of Mortal Sin* (1975), *Schizo* (1976), *The Comeback* (1977), *Home Before Midnight* (1978) and *House of the Long Shadows* (1983). In 1988 he attempted to set up a new film, *Blind Spot*, a crime drama based on a James Hadley Chase novel, but the promised finance didn't materialise. He currently travels the world buying and selling houses, but keeps in touch with many old buddies including Stanley Long and Ray Selfe. He is not the American actor Peter Walker, who appeared in second features in the Fifties; the producer Peter Walker, who was an executive on *The Secret Policeman's Ball* (1979) and other films; nor the exhibitor Peter Walker, who owns the Camden Parkway cinemas in London.

NORMAN J. WARREN

Director Norman J. Warren has been around for ages, but his career has been distinguished by bursts of activity interspersed by years in the wilderness. A lifelong film fanatic, he's been in the business since 1959, when he worked as an assistant to Anatole and Dimitri de Grunwald. 1967: *Her Private Hell*. 1968: *Loving Feeling*. 1976: *Satan's Slave*. 1977: *Prey*. 1978: *Terror*. 1979: *Outer Touch*. 1980: *Inseminoid*. 1984: *Gunpowder*. 1986: *Bloody New Year* a.k.a. *Time Warp Terror*. In between planning two new features (a re-make of the Fifties sci-fi thriller *Fiend Without a Face* and a sequel to *Terror*), Warren has been directing industrial documentaries and a number of promos and educational films for the BBC.

JENNY WESTBROOK

Attractive, bubbly starlet seen in *The Sex Thief* and *Keep It Up Jack!* (both 1973), *Confessions of a Window Cleaner* (1974), *Erotic Inferno* and *Secrets of a Superstud* (both 1975). Both she and her young daughter, Jade, were popular on Benny Hill's TV shows. Jenny married wealthy businessman Andrew Wilson and retired to the country to breed horses.

DONOVAN WINTER

Amiable eccentric Donovan Winter has quietened down in recent years, but the Seventies were greatly enlivened by his unswerving devotion to his own films, his attacks on anyone who begged to differ, and his letters to the press in which he fulminated against the inefficacy of the British film industry. He once physically assaulted the editor of the *Monthly Film Bulletin* for publishing a damning review, and successfully sued Thorn-EMI for failing to distribute his film *Give Us Tomorrow*. He could have become another Michael Winner, but never escaped the B-feature rut. Formerly an actor of matinée idol appearance (he was in *Bullet from the Past* in 1956), he turned to directing with an acceptable second feature, *The Trunk* (1960), and a nudie, *World Without Shame* (1961). He then made several wretched shorts before returning to sex films: *Come Back Peter* a.k.a. *Some Like It Sexy* (1969), *Escort Girls* (1973) and *The Deadly Females* (1976). His last feature was the unreleased thriller *Give Us Tomorrow* (1978) and his last short was *Roller Force* (1980). For most of the Eighties he was in the U.S. writing unsold screenplays. Now back in London, he has completed his memoirs, entitled *The Winters of My Discontent*, and continues to tout his favourite screenplay, *The Scarlet Lady*, a big-budget comedy-thriller.

We shall not see their like again...

INDEX

Adair, Hazel, 75, 103
Adam and Eve, 23
Adventures of a Plumber's Mate, 39, 40, *66*, 108, 120, 121
Adventures of a Private Eye, 40, *85*, 120, 126
Adventures of a Taxi Driver, 40, *46*, 60n, *62*, 106, 108, 110, 120
Adventures of Alison, 90
Alcorn, Joan, *86*
Alison Over the Moon, 97
Allen, Keith, 93
Alvin Purple, 14
American Werewolf in London, An, 96, 101
Andrews, Barry, *82*
Anning, Nick, 90n
Armstrong, Michael, 103-04, 107, 108, 111, 123, 129
Arnold, Jack, 75
Ashby, Debee, 96
Askwith, Robin, 61, 72, 104-05, *109*
Au Pair Girls, 72
Austine, Nicola, 105

Balch, Antony, 19, 68, 71, 105, 128
Bardot, Brigitte, 7, 54, 125
Bass, Alfie, *46*, 48, 49
Bates, Alan, 72
Bayley, Rob, 97
B.B.F.C., 7, 19, 20, 24, 32, 43, 51, 67, 87, 91, 96, 97, 99
Beccarie, Claudine, 14
Behave Yourself, 60
Bennett, Compton, 72
Bennett, Hywel, *74*
Berens, Leslie, 40
Beresford, Al: *see* Long, Stanley
Bergman, Anna, 106

Best, George, 97
Best of Blue Movies: see *Rustler Collection, The*
Best of Electric Blue, The, 93
Bilitis, 14
Bird, Minah, 106
Bird, Walter, 11
Birkin, Jane, 72
Bitch, The, 76
Birth of a Baby, 71,
Birth Without Fear, 71
Blackstone, Tim, 106
Blonde Ambition, 121
Blow Up, 72
Blue Peter, 34, 116
Body Love, 99
Bond, Julia, 106
Bond, Sue, 106
Booth, James, *82*
Bosanquet, Reginald, 93
Bounce, 95
Box, Betty, 127
Bown, John, 68, 107, 129
Bread, 37, 120
Brent, John, *69, 70*
British Board of Film Censors/Classification: see B.B.F.C.
Britton, Mike, *70*
Brook-Partridge, Bernard, 83, 84
Browlie, David, 84
Buzzell, Edward, 27

Cadell, Ava, 107
Campbell, Gavin, *66*
Campbell, Martin, 27, 52, 104, 107-08, 116
Can I Come Too?, 57, 117, 120, 128
Can You Keep It Up For a Week?, 19, 75, 77, *92*, 103, 120, 121

133

Career Girl, 51
Carry On Cleo, 27
Carry On Cowboy, 27
Carry On Nurse, 27
Carry On Regardless, 27, *28*,
Carry On Sergeant, 27, 91
Cashfield, Katy, 23
Chaffey, Don, 20
Chippendales, The, 97
Clegg, Tom, 68
Clinic Xclusive, 75, 103
Club International, 91
Cole, Adam, 91, 93, *100*
Cole, Martin, 40
Collins, Jackie, 75, 76
Collins, Joan, 76
Collins, Pauline, 35, *38*
Color Climax, 88
Come Play With Me, 42, *46*, 48-9, 78, 105, 106, 120, 121, 124
Commuter Husbands, 57, 105, 112, 119
Compton-Cameo, 54, 118, 129
Confessions from the David Galaxy Affair, 77, 78, 111, 124
Confessions of a Window Cleaner, 72, 126, 131
Conway, Carl, *18*, 23, 61
Cooke, Ivor, 90n
Cool it Carol!, 15, 27, 105, 128, 130
Corbett, Harry H., 40
Countess Dracula, 72
Cramer, Ross, 58
Crossroads, 72, 89, 103, 115
Cruel Passion, *74*, 75

Danepak, 97, *100*, 101
Danning, Sybill, 14
Danziger, Edward & Harry, 24
Day, Venicia, *92*
Day With Sarah, A, 91

Deadly Females, The, 67, 131
Deadly Weapons, 14
Deeley, Heather, 57, 108
Deep Throat, 14, 48
Deep Wet Lust, 95
Demme, Jonathan, 75, 85
Deneuve, Catherine, 35
Derek, John, 20, *21*
Deveraux, Monique, *41*
Devonshire, Felicity, 108
Doing the Best I Can, 115
Donaldson, Hilary, 29
Dona Flor and her Two Husbands, 14
Dors, Diana, 40
Drage, Prudence, *66*, 108
Dreamboys, The, 97
Drew, Linzi, *94*, 96, 101
Duncan, Alan, 43
During One Night, 51

Ecstasy, 23
Educating Julie, 97
Ekland, Britt, 93, *94*
Electric Blue, 91, 93, *94*, 95, 96, *98*, 100
Electric Blue - the Movie, 93
Emily, 75
Emmanuelle, 14, 75, 76, 110
Emmanuelle in Soho, *12*, 13, 78, 106, 128
Emney, Fred, 40
Erotic Fantasies (1971), 118
Erotic Fantasies (1978), 112
Erotic Inferno, 108, 126, 128, 131
Eskimo Nell, 27, 104, 107, 108
Evans, Barry, 40, *62*
Everard, John, 11
Eves on Skis, 51, 117
Eves Without Leaves, 11
Exposé, 15, 75, *80*, 117, 118, 126

Fancey, Adrienne, 76, 110, 111, 123
Fancey, E.J., 32, 110-11
Fancey, Malcolm, 76, 110, 111, 123
Fanny Hill (1966), 51
Fanny Hill (1973), 90
Fantasy Manor, 95
Faulkner, Sally, *82*, 111-12
Female Domination, 96
Fiesta, 95
Five of the Best, 121
Flesh Gordon, 14
Flesh is Weak, The, 20, *21*
For Women, 97
Forbidden Women, 20
Ford, Derek, 14, 37, 52, 54, 56, 57-8, 67, 108, 112, 119
Ford, Donald, 52, 54, 56, 119
Forgive Us Our Trespasses, 35
Forsyth, Petrina, *10, 44*
Four Dimensions of Greta, The, 27, 63, *64*, 105, 106, 108, 127, 128, 130
Fox, Samantha, 95
Fraser, John, 35
Fraser, Liz, 40, 99
Freeman, Michael, 13-4, 90-1, 96
French Lessons, 90
Frink, Elizabeth, 51
Fruits of Summer, The, 20
Fry, Stephen, 83
Furie, Sidney J., 51

Games That Lovers Play, 68, *69*, 93, 118
Garden of Eden, The, 20, 23, 24
Gay Man's Guide to Safer Sex, The, 98, 99
Gay, Russell, 29, 95
Geeson, Sally, *50*
George, Susan, 37
Gillespie, Dana, 35

Girl of Shame, 35
Girls Come First, *80*, 108, 111, 112, 115, 120, 123, 129
Glass Table Orgy, 90
Goalen, Barbara, 29
Goddard, Colin, 28
Grant, David, 71, 72, 87, 110, 112-13, 116, 123, 127-28
Great British Striptease, The, 95
Great Rock 'n' Roll Swindle, The, 99, 124
Green, Harry, *28*
Green, Michael, 57, 113
Green, Pamela, *6*, 7-8, *9*, *10*, 11, *31*, 42, *44*, 45, 48, 49, 78, 95, 101, 113, 115, 123
Groupie Girl, 37, 112
Growing Up, 40
Guccione, Bob, 76
Guest, Val, 72
Gypsy Fire, 113

Hallett, Neil, *89*
Hamill, John, 72, 115, *122*
Hamilton, Janie, 96
Handl, Irene, 40, 49, 72
Happy Hooker, The, 14
Hardcastle, Leslie, 83
Hardcore, 75, 108, 115, 126
Hare, Doris, 72
Harper, Marie, 96
Harris, Sidney, 20
Harrison Marks, George, *10*, 27, 29, *41*, 42-3, *44*, 45, *46*, 48-9, 61, 67, 78, 89, *109*, 113, 118, 121, 123, 125, 129
Hart, Diane, 93
Hartford-Davis, Robert, 19, 51-2, 56, 107, 115-16
Hartley, Peter, 87
Hansfrauen-Report, 57
Hayden, Linda, *80*, 118

Hayes, Thomas, 87
Hawtrey, Charles, 27
Health and Efficiency, 11
Hebditch, David, 90n
Helga, 71
Heller, Otto, 8, 43
Hennessey, Paul, 110
Henry, Stephen, 101
Hepworth, Cecil, 43
Her Private Hell, 68, 116, 131
Herbert, Henry, 75
Hicks, Ken, 99
Hills, Gillian, 71
Hitch-Hike, 97
Hollander, Xaviera, 15
Home Before Midnight, 65, 128, 130
Honey, Lindsay, 96
Hot Girls, The, 42n, 106, 107, 121, 127
House of Whipcord, 63, 116, 123, 130
How to Undress in Public Without Undue Embarrassment, 72
Howard, Cathy, *70*
Hughes, Steve, *100*
Hunter, Jackie, 96

I Like Birds, 61, 130
I Love Linzi, *94*
I'm Not Feeling Myself Tonight!, 42n, *82*, 106, 108, 111, 123, 126, 129
Immoral Mr Teas, The, 51
In With Auntie, 95
Initiants, The, 96
International Red Tape, 93
Intimate Confessions of a Chinese Courtesan, 14
Intimate Teenage Secrets: see *It Could Happen to You!*,
Irving, Penny, 116
It Could Happen To You!, 37, 104, 113, 120

Jaeckin, Just, 29
James, Sid, *28*, 127
Jane and Janice Get Them Off, 91
Jarman, Derek, 99
Jessel, Derek, *21*
Jessop, Peter, 61, 116
Jones, Angela, *10*
Jones, Carol, 72
Jones, Mark, 57, 116-17

Kamera, 7, 11, 43
Käpy sellän alla, 71
Karen, Anna, 32
Kaufman, Boris, 20
Kay, Sybilla, *86*, 107
Keatering, Michael, 24, 51, 117
Keeler, Christine, 90
Keep It Up Downstairs, *89*, 103, 120, 124, 125
Keep It Up, Jack!, 57, 112, 113, 117, 120
Kendall, Suzy, *85*
Kenelm Clarke, James, 75, 117-18, 123, 131
Kennedy, Vicky: see Nolan, Margaret
Kerr, Bill, *80*
King Arthur's Lady Returns, 96
Kinky Darlings, The: see *Per una valigia piene di donne*
Klinger, Michael, 35, 52, 54, 58, 111, 118, 129
Kutner, Philip, *28*

Lady Victoria's Training, 90
Lair of the White Worm, The, 96
Lake, Alan, 77
Lamarr, Hedy, 20
Landis, John, 101
Landré, Rita: see Green, Pamela
Laurent, Agnès, 27, *30*
Lavender, Ian, 40
Leigh, Malcolm, 68, 93, 111, 118-19

Leonard, Bridget, *10, 44*
Lesbian She-Males, 96
Let's Be Daring, Madame, 35
Let's Get Laid!, 75, 105, 126
Lewis, Morton, 52, 119
Lewis, Stephen, 40
Lilliput, 11
Linda Lovelace for President, 15
Lindsay, John, 13-4, 42n, 47, 84, 87, 107, 119-20, 123
Lloyd, Stephanie Anne, 96
Lolita James, 91
London in the Raw, 35, *47*
London Knights, The, 97
London Opinion, 11
Long, Stanley, *17*, 20, 26, *28*, 29, 32, 34-5, *36*, 37, 40, 43, *47*, 56, 57, 58, 60n, 61, 67, 85, 99, 104, 110, 111, 116, 118, 119, 120, *122*, 123, 125, 130
Longhurst, Sue, 57, *85*, *114*, 120
Love, Anita, *18*
Love is a Splendid Illusion, 68
Love Pill, The, 42n
Love Variations, 71, 72, 97, 112
Lovelace, Linda, 48
Lovers' Guide, The, 71, 97, 99
Lovers' Guide 2, The, *73*, 99
Loving Feeling, 68, *69, 70*
Lumley, Joanna, 68, *69*, 93
Lusardi, Linda, 95
Lust for a Vampire, 62, 120

Macaskie, Charles, 7, 45, 123
Making Love, 99
Man of Violence, 61, 130
Mandel, Suzy, *46*, 120-21
Manning, Bernard, 95
Marchant, Vic, 96, *100*
Marks, George Harrison: *see* Harrison Marks, George
Marrian, Stephanie, 121

Mary Had a Little, 27, *30* 51
Mary Millington's True Blue Confessions, 78
McGillivray, David, 121, 123
McGrath, Joe, 67, 111, 123
McLaren, Malcolm, 99
McVicar, John, 93
Meadows, Paula, 91
Members Only, 96
Men Only, 11, 43, 91, 126
Meyer, Russ, 14, 29, 51, 58, 130
Miller, Arnold Louis, 27, *28*, 29, 32, 34-5, *36*, 37, 40, 111, 118, 123-24
Miller, Mandy, 78
Miller, Nat, 23-4, 123, 124
Millington, Mary, 19, *46*, 48, *77*, 78, 79, 95, 99, 124, 126
Miss Adventures at Mega Boob Manor, 95
Mondo Cane, 35
Monique, 68, *86*, 107
More About the Language of Love, 71
More Adventures of Alison, 90
Morgan, Chesty, 14
Morrissey, Paul, 99
My Husband in Panties, 96

Naked as Nature Intended, 6, 7, *10*, 19, *31*, 43, 44, 113, 115, 118, 121
Naked World of Harrison Marks, The, 45, 113, 121
Naturist, The, 23
Naughton, David, 101
Naughty!, 37, 119, 120
Naughty Dreams of Miss Owen, The, 96
Negus-Fancey, 103, 111, 118
Neil, Christopher, *66*, *85*
Nelson, Howard, *41*
Never Take Sweets from a Stranger, 51

Nine Ages of Nakedness, The, 42, *44*, 45, *89*, 121
No Sex Please - We're British, 15, 105, 125, 126
Nolan, Margaret, 125
Norwood, Victoria, 99
Nude and Variations, 51
Nudes of the World, *28*, 32, 34
Nudist Memories, 32
Nudist Paradise, *12*, 13, *18*, 23-4, *26*, 32, 51, 124
Nudist Story, The, 24
Nutcracker, 105, 106, 116

O'Hara, Gerry, 67, 90
Oliver, Anthony, 24
On the Game, 37, *39*, 105, 120
100% Lust, 90n
One Summer of Happiness, 20
Opel, Robert, 97
Outram, Bernice, 95
Owen, Stacey, 95

Page, Betty, 43
Paige, Elaine, 39, 40
Paris Playgirls: see *Svenska flickor i Paris*
Park Lane, 76
Pascal, Françoise, 68, *69*, *89*, 110, 125, 126
Pattern of Evil, *41*, 121
Patterson, Paula, *70*
Paul Raymond's Erotica, 75
Payne, Cynthia, 90
Pécas, Max, 14
Peeping Tom, 8, 43, 113
Penthouse, 91, 96
Per una valigia piene di donne, 71
Percy, 72, *74*, 127
Perfect Exposure, 97
Permissive, 128

Personal Services, 90
Pertwee, Jon, 40
Peters, Luan, 61, *62*
Phillips, Evan, 13
Photo Studio, 29
Pink Orgasm, 108, 112
Pitt, Ingrid, 72
Playbirds, The, *66*, 78, 79, 121, 124
Pleasure Principle, The, 90
Polanski, Roman, 35, 54, 118, 129
Pollard, Su, 95
Porn Brokers, The, 42n
Porn Gold, 90n
Powell, Michael, 8
Poynter, Roy, 7
Primitive London, 35, *38*
Pritchard, Hilary, 125-26
Private Spy, 93
Promise of Bed, A, *17*, 37, 112

Queen of the Blues, 78, 105, 124
Question of Adultery, A, 20

Raunchy Randy Ravers, 91
Raymond, Paul, 75, 88, 91, 126
Reed, Oliver, 72
Reeves, Michael, 37, 40, 54, 129
Reluctant Nudist, The, 21, *30*, 51
Repulsion, 35, 118
Respectable Prostitute, The, 20
Response, 95
Rice-Davies, Mandy, 90
Richardson, Iseult, 123
Richmond, Fiona, 75, *80*, 95, 105, *109*, 117, 126
Rilla, Wolf, 75
Ringwald, Monika, *114*, 126
Rise and Fall of Ivor Dickie, The, 96
Robbins, Derek, 67
Robinson, Cardew, 48
Rogers, Peter, 27, 126-27

Rollin, Jean, 14
Rosenberg, Max J., 24
Rowles, Kenneth, 56
Roye, 11
Rushton, William, 40
Russell, Ken, 72, 96
Rustler Connoisseur's Collection, The, 95

Sainsbury, Timothy, 87
Salt, Jackie, *10, 44*
Samuels, Stuart, 42, 45
Sarno, Joe, 14
Saturday Night Out, 53, 54, 115
Saunders, Charles, 23
Scandal, 90
School for Sex, 60, 61, 65, 125, 130
Screw Loose, 90
Sebastiane, 99
Secrets of a Door to Door Salesman, 75, *85,* 108, 111, 112, 120
Secrets of a Superstud, 52n, 108, 117, 119, 129, 131
Secrets of a Windmill Girl, 35, *38*
Secrets of Sex, 70, 71, 105, 106, 128
Selfe, Ray, 57, 111, 123, 127-28, 130
Selwyn, Alan, 112
Sen, Bachoo, 68, 116, 128
Seventeen, 14
Sex Can Be Difficult, 35
Sex Express, 57, 106, 108, 112
Sex Play, 75
Sex Thief, The, 86, 104, 107, 131
Sexy Secrets of the Kissogram Girls, 91
Sexy Secrets of the Sex Therapist, The, 96
Shonteff, Lindsay, 67, 128
Simonds, Charlie, 97
Sinclair, Peter, 99, 116
Sinderella, 112

Singleton, Valerie, 34
Sins of Youth, 35
Skin Skin: see *Käpy sellän alla*
Skoog, Lena, 63
Slaney, Walter, 51
Small, Tina, 95
Smith, Murray, 61, 128-29
Snow White and the Seven Perverts, 112
Solitaire, 91
Some Like it Cool, 22, 24, 32, 111
Sparrow, Bobby, 129
Spielplatz, 7, 23, 32, 123
Stag Films, 31, 32
Stag Night, 95
Stanway, Andrew, 97
Stark, Koo, *74,* 75
Stork, 14
Streaker!, 97
Strip Poker, 61, 130
Stross, Raymond, 20
Stuart, Sam: *see* Samuels, Stuart
Stud, The, 15, 76, 106
Subotsky, Milton J., 24
Suburban Wives, 57, 105, 112
Sullivan, David, 48, 49, 76, 78, 95, 96, 129
Sun and Health, 11
Sunswept, 24, 117
Super Stagarama, 95
Supervirility, 99
Svenska flickor i Paris, 52
Sykes, Peter, 43

Take an Easy Ride, 56
Take Off Your Clothes and Live, 19, 34, 51
Taylor, Gilbert, 35
Taylor, Larry, 57n
Tenser, Tony, 52, 54, 57, 104, 107, 111, 118, 129-30

That Kind of Girl, 24
Thérèse and Isabelle, 14
Thomas, Erroll, 87
Tiffany Jones, 63, 130
Titanic Toni, 95
To Rio For Love, 116
Too Young to Love, 51
Top Secret, 93
Torday, Terry, 14
Tracey, Derek, 72
Trevelyan, John, 24, 25, 31, 43, 45, 57, 123, 130
Truth or Dare, 90
Turkish Delight, 14

Unbelievable Experience, 95

Vampire Lovers, The, 72

Walker, Edward Craven: *see* Keatering, Michael
Walker, Gloria, *86*
Walker, Pete, 27, 29, 42, 58, *59*, 60-3, 65, 67, 104-05, *109*, 110, 111, 116, 123, 125, 130
Walton, Kent, 75, 103
Warbeck, David, *86*
Warren, Norman J., 68, *114*, 123, 125, 127, 128, 131
Watling, Jack, 27, *30*
Wattis, Richard, 72
Webb, Douglas, 113, 115
Webb, Rita, 48
West End Jungle, 32, *33*
Westbrook, Jenny, 131
What the Censor Saw, 24
What's Good for the Goose, 50, 54, 125
What's Up Nurse, 57, 106, 108, 112, 113, 126
What's Up Superdoc, 57, 105, 106, 112, 113, 124
Whitehouse, 48, 76
Whitehouse, Mary, 40
Whitehouse Video Show No.1, 95
Wife Swappers, The, 14, 37, *55*, 56-7, 112
Wilkinson, June, 51
Williams, Kenneth, 99
Window Dresser, The, 8, *9,* 113
Windmill Theatre, 29, 35
Winner, Michael, 24, 32, 60, 111, 131
Winter, Donovan, 67, 131
Wisdom, Norman, 43, *50,* 54
Witches' Brew, 113
Women in Love, 72
World is Full of Married Men, The, 76, 105, 110, 111
Wynn, Pat, 95

Xcitement, 113

Yannick, 24
Yellow Teddybears, The, 24, *25,* 51, *53,* 54, 56, 65, 115
Yes Girls, The, 128
You're Driving Me Crazy!, 112, 116, 121, 128

Zeta, 95
Zeta's Sexy Video Show, 95

David McGillivray produces, directs, writes and performs for stage, screen, radio and television. He is also a journalist, critic, broadcaster and professional film buff who has answered readers' questions for various film magazines, including *Films & Filming, Film Review* and *Shivers*, since 1971. He saw most of the films discussed in this book while he was writing for the British Film Institute's *Monthly Film Bulletin* (1970-1982). He has contributed to several books, e.g. *A Heritage of Horror* (1973), *The Encyclopaedia of Rock* (1976), *International Film Guide* (1976-79), *Anatomy of the Movies* (1981), *The Film Yearbook* (1983-86), *Sore Throats and Overdrafts* (1988) and *Shock Xpress 1* (1991), and since 1987 he has been the editor of the *British Alternative Theatre Directory*. But this is the first book he has written by himself.

Author's photograph by Michael Hoyle.